TARGET
Reading Comprehension

TARGET

Reading Comprehension

Essential Reading for Effective Learning

For Class Teachers, SENCOs and
Support for Learning Staff

Bernadette McLean
and Rosie Wood

Helen Arkell Dyslexia Centre
Barrington Stoke

First published 2004 in Great Britain by Barrington Stoke Ltd,
Sandeman House, Trunk's Close, 55 High Street, Edinburgh, EH1 1SR

www.barringtonstoke.co.uk

ISBN 1-84299-161-2

Editor: Julia Rowlandson

Original cover idea by Stuart Boyde

Designed and typeset by GreenGate Publishing Services, Tonbridge
Printed in China by Sino Publishing House Ltd

Contents

For simplicity, in this book the student will be referred to as 'he' and the teacher as 'she'.

Introduction

Target Reading Comprehension provides a systematic set of activities for teachers and classroom assistants to use to improve a reader's comprehension of the written word.

Target Reading Accuracy is the companion volume offering practical tips and activities to promote accurate and rapid word recognition.

There are activities suitable for struggling readers at upper primary and secondary levels.

Each book contains the comprehensive checklist which directs you to appropriate starting points for individual readers.

What you will find in this book

- **A system** to enable readers to read with more understanding.

- **The next stage** from *Target Reading Accuracy.**
  When readers read with accuracy they have mental energy to think about and understand what they have read. Reading accuracy must come first.

- **Assessment** to determine breakdown points in the reading comprehension task and where to begin with reading remediation.

- **A Checklist for the teacher** to use whilst the pupil is reading.

---

* McLean, B. and Wood, R. (2004) Target Reading Accuracy. Barrington Stoke

- **A Guide for teachers and classroom assistants** to find the appropriate sections in this book, and in *Target Reading Accuracy*, to provide the necessary support.

- **A photocopiable checklist for the reader to use** with teacher support to pinpoint his reading difficulties (see Chapter 10 – Reader's Toolkit).

- **Individualised teaching points** in the form of a skill-building programme with teaching ideas and ways to encourage comprehension.

- **Photocopiable sheets** with activities for readers to carry out independently or with support.

- **A structured approach** working from word meaning, through sentences to text level.

- **Target cards** which prompt activities for readers to carry out independently or with support. These can be linked to individual Education Plans. There is a template for teachers' own use on page 13.

This book aims to improve reading skills so that readers are competent to tackle all texts.

Types of reading that are needed at this stage

By this stage, teachers need to ensure that readers will have the following skills across the curriculum. Readers need to be able to:

- scan for a particular piece of information

- skim text for a 'general idea' of content

- read questions and instructions

- read for information

- recall what has been read

- distinguish fact and opinion

- understand literal and figurative language

- infer meaning and be able to read between the lines

- be able to predict what comes next

- determine key points

- evaluate and criticise written text

- understand the writer's purpose.

In truth, because poor readers avoid reading, these skills have not developed. Experts believe in the 'Matthew Effect'.* Poor readers read less and so become poorer readers. The 'Matthew Effect' means that in reading (as in life), the rich get richer and the poor get poorer. If students do not read, they lose the opportunity to gain vocabulary, background knowledge and information about how text is structured. This means that they bring poorer skills to the reading task and find it even harder. On the other hand, good readers improve vocabulary, gain knowledge and build up awareness of the structure of texts. They can then become even better readers.

* Stanovich, K.E. (2000) *Progress in Understanding Reading: Scientific Foundations and New Frontiers*. New York: Guilford Press. ISBN 1 5723 0565 7

What reading is:

- Effective readers read with accuracy, at a reasonable speed, understand what they are reading and recall the read material once the reading activity is over.

- Effective readers use 'bottom-up' strategies to support reading and 'top-down' strategies to monitor and check accuracy and understanding.

Bottom-up starts with learning about letter/sound links and using phonics. This is the approach used in *Target Reading Accuracy*.

Top-down uses knowledge of grammar and meaning to help predict words. This is the approach used in *Target Reading Comprehension*.

- Reading is a learned skill that needs to be taught: *'Reading is not a natural activity, but a set of gradually acquired component skills learned independently, but later integrated and automated ... There is no single straight path to competence in reading ...'* (Turner, 1995)*

See Appendix on page 180 for 'Normal development of reading'.

See Appendix on page 182 for 'Reading tests'.

---

* Turner, M. (1995) 'Children learn to read by being taught', in Owen, P. and Pumfrey, P.D. (eds) *Children Learning to Read*, Vol. 1. Basingstoke: Falmer Press.

What you need for reading

- Good eyesight and good hearing which lead to good visual processing and the ability to learn about sounds in words.

- Experience and knowledge of the world.

- Good language skills:
  - a wide vocabulary
  - mastery of grammatical constructions in spoken language
  - good understanding of spoken language.

- Awareness of concepts of print:
  - directionality of words from left to right and moving from one line to the next
  - orientation of letters which are easily confused, e.g. *b/d, u/n, m/w, t/f, p/q*
  - the same letter in different forms, e.g. a, A, a, **A**
  - sequence of letters and words, e.g. *on/no, saw/was, the dog bit the man/the man bit the dog*
  - letter/sound links, e.g. *c = /k/ or /s/, ea* as in *seat, break, bread.*

Pages 7–11 are a guide for teachers and classroom assistants on where to start with reading remediation. Use this with the photocopiable checklist which is on page 12.

Select a sufficiently challenging text, i.e. 90–95% words are easy to read. If the text is too easy, difficulties will not become apparent. If it is too difficult, the reader will become frustrated and have a poor understanding of what he is reading.

Fill in the checklist on page 12 as you listen to the student read.

20 Questions

Guide for teachers and classroom assistants on where to start with reading remediation

Listen to the reader reading text at a sufficiently challenging level, i.e. 90–95% of words are easy to read. If the text is too easy to read, difficulties will not be apparent. If it is too difficult, it will be at frustration level and the reader will have poor understanding of what he is reading.

The following is a guide to help you to fill in the checklist (page 12) and to decide where to begin with remediation. References are to this book (TRC, *Target Reading Comprehension*) and TRA, *Target Reading Accuracy*.

Questions to ask	Think about …	Action to take	References
1 Is he reluctant to tackle reading tasks?	This may be because he lacks confidence because he has failed in the past.	Check reading level of text. If it is too hard, try easier text. See Chapter 6.	Ch. 6 TRA 'Readability'
		Check knowledge of high frequency words.	Ch. 4 TRA 'Word Reading'
2 Is he willing to try if he does not know a word?	If not, he may be lacking in confidence as above, or he may still be at an early reading development stage.	Build phonological awareness and word attack strategies.	Ch. 3 TRA 'Phonological Awareness and Phonics' Ch. 4 TRA 'Word Reading'
3 Does he use the letters in the word to help sound out an unfamiliar word?	If not, he may not be linking the letter strings with sounds.	Teach phonological awareness and decoding.	Ch. 3 TRA 'Phonological Awareness and Phonics'

Cont'd

	Questions to ask	Think about ...	Action to take	References
4	Does he have difficulty with longer words?	He may not have word attack skills due to difficulties with phonological awareness or a lack of understanding of the structure of words, e.g. revisiting where *re* is the prefix, *visit* is the root word and *ing* is the suffix.	Build phonological awareness and teach the structure of words, e.g. prefixes, root words, suffixes.	Ch. 3 TRA *'Phonological Awareness and Phonics'* Ch. 4 TRA *'Word Reading'* Ch. 3 TRC *'Word Reading – Vocabulary Extension'*
5	Does he lack fluency when he reads?	He may be having to work out or sound out too many words.	Build up automaticity at word level beginning with high frequency words.	Ch. 4 TRA *'Word Reading'*
6	Are his substitutions not real words?	There may be an underlying spoken language difficulty. He may have a poor vocabulary.	Develop a larger and more flexible vocabulary.	Ch. 3 TRC *'Word Reading – Vocabulary Extension'*
7	Do real word substitutions make sense in the context?	He may be over-reliant on the context at the expense of accurate decoding.	Develop decoding skills.	Ch. 3 TRA *'Phonological Awareness and Phonics'*
8	Do real word substitutions **not** make sense in the context?	He may not be monitoring the sense of the word within the whole sentence.	Teach whole sentence comprehension.	Ch. 4 TRC *'Sentences'*
9	Does he rarely or never self-correct?	He may not be monitoring his comprehension as he reads.	Help him to develop ways of monitoring his understanding while he is reading.	Ch. 8 TRC *'Interactive Reading'*

Cont'd

Questions to ask	Think about ...	Action to take	References
10 What use does he make of pictorial or other visual clues in the text?	1 If he does not use them he may have visual processing problems. 2 If he is over-reliant on visual information it may indicate a lack of reading fluency or the level of text is too difficult.	1 Check visual processing and consider referral. 2 Build up automaticity at word level beginning with high frequency words. Check level of text.	*Ch. 5 TRA 'Visual Processing'* *Ch. 4 TRA 'Word Reading'* *Ch. 6 TRA 'Readability'*
11 Does he read word by word without grouping words into phrases?	He may lack sufficient fluency in reading words and phrases.	Build automaticity at word level. Build phrase-reading ability.	*Ch. 4 TRA 'Word Reading'* *Ch. 4 TRC 'Sentences'*
12 Does he repeat words and/ or phrases?	This may indicate: 1 a memory problem or 2 a visual scanning problem.	1 Teach visualisation skills. 2 Check visual processing and consider referral.	*Ch. 9 TRC 'Visualisation'* *Ch. 5 TRA 'Visual Processing'*
13 Does he have difficulty with left to right scanning and keeping his place? Does he hold the book at an unusual angle or very close to his eyes? Does he screw up his eyes? Does he finger point? Does he leave out or add little words?	Any or all of these may indicate visual processing problems.	Check visual processing and refer for optometric assessment.	*Ch. 5 TRA 'Visual Processing'*

Cont'd

Questions to ask	Think about …	Action to take	References
14 Does he notice punctuation?	If not, this may indicate: 1 a visual processing problem 2 a comprehension problem because he is not attending to phrase and sentence boundaries.	1 Check visual processing. 2 Develop comprehension skills starting at sentence level and moving to longer pieces of text.	*1 Ch. 5 TRA 'Visual Processing'* 2 Ch. 4 TRC 'Sentences' Ch. 5 TRC 'Paragraphs and Longer Texts'
15 Does he read too quickly?	He may be a skimmer, not attending to detail in the text.	Teach him how to notice detail in text.	*Ch. 4 TRA 'Word Reading (Bingo Lookalike words and Snap)* Ch. 4 TRC 'Sentences' (Order of words, Yes/No/Maybe and Same or Different)
16 Does he read too slowly?	1 He may be a plodder, working out the majority of words because he is unable to read words at sight. 2 He does not know when or how to skim read. 3 He may be focusing on decoding skills at the expense of comprehension.	1 Build automaticity at word level beginning with high frequency words. 2 Teach reading strategies to suit purposes of reading. 3 Teach comprehension skills starting at sentence level.	*1 Ch. 4 TRA 'Word Reading'* 2 Ch. 7 TRC 'Types of Reading' 3 Ch. 4 TRC 'Sentences' Ch. 5 TRC 'Paragraphs and Longer Texts'
17 Does he read accurately but with little comprehension or recall of the text once the reading activity is over?	He may be a passive reader who is not interacting with the text.	Teach ways of interacting with text and how to visualise.	Ch 8 TRC 'Interactive Reading' Ch 9 TRC 'Visualisation'

Cont'd

Questions to ask	Think about …	Action to take	References
18 Does he find the vocabulary or the concepts too difficult?	1 He may not know the words. 2 He may lack familiarity with the topic.	1 Help extend his vocabulary. 2 Build familiarity with the topic before reading. 3 Teach KWL and SKWL.	1 *Ch. 3 TRC 'Word Reading – Vocabulary Extension'* 2 *Ch. 6 TRC 'Listening to Reading'* 3 *Ch. 8 TRC 'Interactive Reading' (KWL and SKWL)*
19 Does he read all texts in the same way?	He may lack the necessary flexibility to adjust his approach dependent on the reason for reading.	Teach different strategies for reading and when to use them.	*Ch. 7 TRC 'Types of Reading'*
20 Does he enjoy reading?	If not, he may be reading books that are too easy or too difficult.	Check reading level. Teach him how to choose the right level.	*Ch. 6 TRA 'Readability'* *Ch. 6 TRC 'Listening to Reading'*

20 QUESTIONS CHECKLIST

20 questions to ask:	Yes/ No	Comments:
1 Is he reluctant to tackle reading tasks?		
2 Is he willing to try if he does not know a word?		
3 Does he use the letters in the word to help sound out an unfamiliar word?		
4 Does he have difficulty with longer words?		
5 Does he lack fluency when he reads?		
6 Are his substitutions not real words?		
7 Do real word substitutions make sense in the context?		
8 Do real word substitutions not make sense in the context?		
9 Does he rarely or never self-correct?		
10 Does he use pictorial or other visual clues in the text?		
11 Does he read word by word without grouping words into phrases?		
12 Does he repeat words and/or phrases?		
13 Does he have difficulty with left to right scanning and keeping his place? Does he hold the book at an unusual angle or very close to his eyes? Does he screw up his eyes? Does he finger point? Does he leave out or add little words?		
14 Does he notice punctuation?		
15 Does he read too quickly?		
16 Does he read too slowly?		
17 Does he read accurately but with little comprehension or recall of the text once the reading activity is over?		
18 Does he find the vocabulary or the concepts too difficult?		
19 Does he read all texts in the same way?		
20 Does he enjoy reading?		

Introduction to Comprehension

The ultimate aim of reading is to make sense of the text. For easy understanding, decoding has to be automatic so that the reader's mental effort can focus on the message. There are many reasons why readers may be poor at comprehension:

- poor decoding skills – they may not be able to read the words
- poor vocabulary – they may not be able to understand the words
- poor language skills – they may not pick up clues from the text.

For true comprehension the reader has to do more than decode; he needs to:

- know the vocabulary

- understand the vocabulary in context

- understand the grammatical order of words

- comprehend the literal meaning

- distinguish the important message, i.e. what the main idea is, what is relevant, and what is less relevant

- be able to pick up clues from the text

- recognise the author's point of view

- distinguish fact from opinion

- remember earlier words in order to process them with later ones

- recognise ambiguous phrases and sentences,

  e.g.   It is too hot to eat (weather or food might be too hot)

- recognise if key information is missing

- relate content to knowledge of the world

- have strategies for when comprehension is failing.

Levels of comprehension

The National Literacy Strategy refers to three levels of comprehension:

1 Literal

This is when the answer to the comprehension question is clearly stated in the text.

2 Inferential

There are different kinds of inferential comprehension where the reader needs to infer meaning:

- connecting information from different parts of the text
- bringing general knowledge to the reading activity.

3 Evaluative

This is where the reader expresses his own opinion in:

- drawing conclusions
- considering the author's viewpoint
- predicting outcomes.

Areas of difficulty with comprehension

These can be at word level, sentence level, or text level. Testing comprehension can be carried out formally or informally.

If carrying out a formal comprehension test, check which levels of comprehension the test is probing. For example, is it just a literal recalling of facts, or does it need more thinking and prior knowledge?

If testing informally, check the different levels yourself.

Comprehension is best tested when:

- decoding is fluent

- questions are asked verbally and students do not have to write answers

- students are prompted to give more information if the first response is sketchy or unclear.

Investigate and record differences in response to:

- reading silently or aloud

- re-reading or answering without looking back at the text.

You can then advise on what is useful for individuals.

Effective strategies include:

- increasing vocabulary in spoken language before written language

- improving understanding of figurative language i.e. language that has a meaning not obvious and literal, e.g. *pull his leg*, *struck dumb*, *caught my eye*

- using different types of reading: skimming, scanning, careful reading, interactive reading according to the purpose (see Chapter 7 'Types of Reading' and Chapter 8 'Interactive Reading')

- teaching readers strategies for working independently, such as prediction, using context, guessing, re-reading, reading ahead, determining the purpose of reading

- using cloze procedure to encourage reading for meaning

- sequencing at sentence and text level

- finding key points at sentence and paragraph level

- visualising to assist comprehension

- monitoring comprehension, first by the teacher and then by the reader

- using note-making strategies (mind maps, key words, etc.).

To assess comprehension

If you need detailed information about your reader's comprehension, use the tasks in this chapter. Otherwise use the 20 Questions Guide on page 7 to find where to begin.

1 Decide what type of comprehension you wish to assess (see page 15):
   - literal
   - inferential
   - evaluative.

2 Check the reading passage is at the correct level and can be decoded easily. Refer to *Target Reading Accuracy Chapter 6 'Readability'*, or check that your reader can read easily at least 90% of the words on the passage, and preferably 95%.

3 For beginning or struggling readers use narrative (story) texts.

4 For advanced readers use more complex texts and non-fiction.

Narrative comprehension

In this task, the questions test whether the reader can put the story into his own words, as well as the three levels of comprehension:

- literal

- inferential

- evaluative.

(See page 15 for definitions.)

Instructions

Choose a passage from Photocopiable Sheets 1 or 3 which is well within his reading ability. Photocopiable Sheet 1 is easier than Photocopiable Sheet 3.

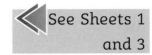 See Sheets 1 and 3

- Ask him to read it silently.

- When he finishes, ask him to give you the main points.

- Use the appropriate record sheet (Photocopiable Sheets 2 or 4) to record his response.

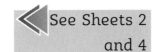 See Sheets 2 and 4

- Keep this on file; use later to check progress.

- Stop at the literal comprehension questions if these are proving too difficult.

If the reader has great difficulty, go back to the 20 Questions Guide in Chapter 1 to determine where to begin.

Non-fiction comprehension

Assess the three levels of comprehension: literal, inferential and evaluative (see page 15 for definitions).

Instructions

Choose a non-fiction passage from a textbook which is well within your reader's reading ability. Photocopiable Sheets 5 and 7 may be used if appropriate.

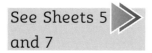
See Sheets 5 and 7

- Ask him to read the passage silently.

- When finished, ask him questions. Start with easy questions of literal understanding. Use questions beginning with:

What?	How?	Where?	Which?
When?	Who?	Why?	

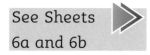
See Sheets 6a and 6b

For the passage on Photocopiable Sheet 5 there are examples of literal and inferential and evaluative questions on Photocopiable Sheets 6a and 6b.

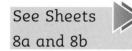
See Sheets 8a and 8b

- For the passage on Photocopiable Sheet 7 there are examples of literal questions on Photocopiable Sheet 8a, and inferential and evaluative questions on Photocopiable Sheet 8b.

- Keep a record on file to check progress.

- If this task is difficult for the reader, go back to the 20 Questions Guide in Chapter 1 to determine where to begin.

Non-fiction comprehension with recall

Do this exercise at a later date in order to check recall as well as understanding.

Instructions

- Use the chosen passage with words deleted. See Photocopiable Sheets 9 and 10.

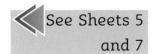
See Sheets 9 and 10

- Ask the reader to read silently.

- Then ask him to work out the words that are missing.

- Record the words for him if he wishes.

- Look at the complete passages on Photocopiable Sheets 5 and 7 to check responses. Accept alternative words if they fit in with the overall meaning and grammar.

See Sheets 5 and 7

- If this is not easy it suggests that reading has been superficial and the reader needs to learn more effective ways of understanding the text. He will benefit from Chapters 5, 7 and 8.

Level 1: The Park

Read the following passage and then tell your teacher the main points in order.

The playground's in a corner of the park, through the side entrance, and up a tarmac path. It's not bad down there. Me and Josh go all the time.

My big mistake was to ask Mum if we could go. She was in the kitchen, sitting at the table, yawning her head off over a cup of coffee, and Jamie was sitting on the floor, muttering on and on to himself as he shunted a conker round the carpet, pretending it was a fire engine or something. I know. Pathetic.

'Go to the playground?' said Mum, smiling at me so hard I got suspicious straight away. 'What a good idea. You can take Jamie with you in the buggy. He's bound to go off to sleep. Up half the night, poor little thing, with his new tooth coming through. Kept me awake till half past three. If I don't have a bit of peace and quiet this afternoon I'm going to murder someone.'

'Take Jamie?' I said backing away. 'To the playground? Mum, you've got to be joking.'

But she wasn't.

So that was it. That was my day ruined. I felt a sort of stone sinking down inside me at the thought of it. Who in their right mind wants to be seen pushing a kid around in a buggy?*

---

* Elizabeth Laird, *The Ice Cream Swipe*, Oxford University Press. ISBN 0-19-275276-6

Narrative Comprehension

Record Sheet

Pupil's name: _____ Date: _____

Level 1: The Park

The exercise on Photocopiable Sheet 1 asks the pupil to summarise the main points. Check which points he has given you.

- The two boys want to go to the park.
- One of them asks his mum.
- She is tired.
- She asks him to take his little brother with him so she can have a rest.
- He is upset because he does not want anyone to see him pushing a child in a buggy.

If they have omitted facts, ask specific questions, e.g.

- What did the boys want to do?
- Who did they ask?
- What is wrong with the boys' mum?
- What does Mum ask them to do?
- Why is the boy upset?

Notice how easily the questions are answered and how long it takes the reader to find the information in the text if it has been recalled.

All the questions up to now check out literal comprehension.

STOP HERE IF THE READER IS HAVING DIFFICULTY.

If literal comprehension seems satisfactory, check higher levels of comprehension. Use the following extension activity.

Cont'd

Extension Activity: Do You Think?

Include the following questions which test comprehension at higher levels. The students have to think more about the information.

The frequent use of the phrase '**do you think**' is to alert the reader to the fact that he has to **think** in order to work out the answer.

Encourage full answers for maximum score.

1 What age do you think Jamie is? 2 months, 1 year or 4 years? Give reasons for your answer. *(4 marks)*

2 Why did Mum's smile make the boy suspicious? *(3 marks)*

3 What do you think shunted means? *(2 marks)*

4 Why do you think Mum was yawning? *(2 marks)*

5 What was 'the sort of stone sinking down inside the narrator'? *(3 marks)*

6 Why do you think that the story teller does not want to take Jamie out? *(2 marks)*

Score out of 16.

Level 2: Alice and Kim

Read the following passage and then tell your teacher the main points in order.

Alice and Kim wanted to go shopping. but they did not have any money. They asked their mother for some pocket money. Their mother refused. She said, 'You got your pocket money already this week and I never let Harry have his pocket money in advance.' She was unwilling to give them the next week's pocket money because she knew, from experience, that they would spend it all at once.

Alice and Kim decided that all they could do was to offer to help around the house to get some money. They talked about the jobs they would each do. Alice asked her mother if she could wash the kitchen floor and hoover and dust the living room. Kim said she would empty the dishwasher and unload the washing machine and hang the clothes out on the line.

Their mother agreed to give them each some money for these jobs. She said that she would let them know how much they would get when they had done their jobs.

Narrative Comprehension

Record Sheet

Pupil's name: _____ **Date:** _____

Level 2: Alice and Kim

The exercise on Photocopiable Sheet 3 asks the pupil to summarise the main points. Check which points he has given you.

- Alice and Kim want to go to the shops.
- They have no money.
- They ask their mother for pocket money.
- Mother says no.
- They offer to do jobs.
- Alice will wash the kitchen floor and hoover and dust the living room.
- Kim will empty the dishwasher and hang out the clothes from the washing machine.
- Mother agrees to give them money.
- She says she will tell them how much when they have done the jobs.

If they have omitted facts do ask specific questions e.g.

- Where did Alice and Kim want to go?
- Why could they not go?
- What do they do next?
- Does their mother agree to give them money?
- What do they think would be a good way to get some money?
- What jobs will each do?
- Does their mother agree?
- When do they know how much they will earn?

Notice how easily the questions are answered and how long it takes the reader to find the information in the text, if it has not been recalled.

All the questions up to now have been checking out **literal comprehension**.

> **Stop here if the reader is having difficulty.**

If literal comprehension seems satisfactory, check higher levels of comprehension (see activity on page 27: 'Do you Think?').

Level 2: Alice and Kim
Extension Activity: Do You Think?

Include the following questions, which test comprehension at higher levels. The students have to think more about the information.

The frequent use of the phrase '**do you think**' is to alert the reader to the fact that he has to **think** in order to work out the answer.

Encourage full answers for maximum score.

1	**Why** did their mother not give them the pocket money they asked for?	2
2	What **do you think** the phrase 'from experience' means?	2
3	What relationship **do you think** there is between Alice and Mary?	1
4	Who **do you think** Harry is?	1
5	How **do you think** Alice and Kim should plan their work if the dishwasher and washing machine are both in the kitchen?	5
6	Which of the two girls, Alice or Kim, **do you think** prefers cleaning jobs?	1
7	Why **do you think** their mother said that she would wait until the work was done before she would let them know how much money they would get?	2
8	How reasonable **do you think** their mother was?	6

Score out of 20.

Summary notes on how well pupil has responded:

Non-fiction Comprehension

Level 1: Second World War

Read the following passage and your teacher will ask you some questions about it.

In the Second World War the British people became healthier. Children from poor families were given meals at school and had milk, orange juice and cod liver oil. There were more jobs for adults who were also given meals at work. People ate less fat and sugar and only had meat once a week. Everyone could only buy small amounts of cheese, tea and eggs. Oranges and bananas, which came from abroad, were very hard to buy and so was chocolate. In 1942 ice cream was banned.

It was important to collect scrap metal, paper and wool. Children got medals for collecting scrap like old keys and books. People even gave the iron railings from their garden fences and the street outside their houses. The recycled metal was used to make planes. Nothing was thrown away.

It was hard to buy new clothes. People had to wear second hand clothes. They mended anything they could. Some women painted a black line down the backs of their legs to look like they had stockings with seams on.

Food was grown everywhere. You could see vegetables growing on school playing fields and in parks. Children went to the country to help with the harvest at the end of the summer. It was a good idea to have hens in your garden so you had your own supply of eggs.

Level 1: Second World War

Examples of questions at a literal level.

1. When did the British become healthier?

2. What did poor children have?

3. What kinds of food could you only buy small amounts of?

4. When was ice cream banned?

5. Why was metal collected?

6. What did people do when they could not buy new clothes?

Use the same language as the passage to make the questions easy or make the questions more challenging by changing the wording, for example:

7. What food was not allowed?

8. What food was scarce?

9. Why and how were children rewarded?

Level 1: Second World War

Examples of questions at higher levels (inferential and evaluative)

10 Which of the following opinions do you think the author of this passage would agree with

    a   Children became lazy during the war   true/false

    b   Not having enough food was a bad thing   true/false

    c   If you had a lot of money you could buy
       anything you wanted   true/false

    d   Everyone made an effort to help with shortages
       during the war   true/false

11 Find a word in the passage that means the same as 'forbidden'.
    (Notice how well the reader can skim for the answer.)

12 Find a word in the passage that means the same as 'repaired'.
    (Notice how well the reader can skim for the answer.)

13 Why did people become more healthy? Was it because:

    ●   They got rid of all their rubbish?

    ●   More adults worked?

    ●   People ate less meat, sugar and fat?

**Check comprehension and recall of Sheet 5 on a later occasion using
Sheet 9.**

Level 2: The African Famine

Read the following passage and your teacher will ask you some questions about it:

The African countries have to borrow money from rich countries and from banks. Every year they have to pay more money back to the rich countries. They cannot spend money on their own people because they have to pay the rich countries. Often they cannot pay the rich countries, so they have to borrow more money. So things get worse. And worse.

There are other problems too. In some parts of these countries there are no roads. There have been wars in Ethiopia, Sudan and Chad for many years. Governments spend money on the wrong things.

Aid agencies and the Ethiopian government knew that a famine was coming. They knew this in 1983, a year before the famine came. But the Ethiopian government seemed to do nothing. Nobody listened to the aid agencies, and the rich countries did nothing.

In 1984 the rains did not come.

When people started dying, the television cameras arrived. The TV pictures shocked the world. When the world realised what was happening, aid poured in to Ethiopia. But it was too late for many people. Thirty million people were starving and one million died.

Cont'd

In 1985 there was plenty of rain. Farmers could grow food again. But there was still no answer to all the real problems. 1988 was another dry year and famine returned. A lot of aid givers realised that their money had not really changed anything. It had helped people to stay alive but the problems were still there. These problems will not go away until the rich countries change their ideas. The rich countries buy many things from the poor countries, but they pay the lowest possible prices. Then the rich countries sell things to the poor countries at very high prices. So it is impossible for the poor countries to grow stronger and richer.

Aid is not used carefully enough. People are not always asked what help they need. So they get the wrong kind of help.

Aid must be given to the right people too. It must be given to the small farmers. In Africa, women do 80% of the farming work; but only 2% of aid money is given to women farmers.

Lastly, people from rich countries must tell their governments to give more aid to the poorer countries of the world. They should give more aid because the people in those countries need it. But it would also be good for the rich countries. If the poor countries were stronger and richer they could buy more things from the rich countries. That would be good for everybody. As Bob said to the European Parliament, 'You need Africa as much as they need you'.*

---

* Bob Geldof: The pop star who raised £70 million for famine relief in Ethiopia by Charlotte Gray, LDA edition written by D'Arcy Adrian-Vallance, Cambridge, 1989

Level 2: The African Famine

When your pupil has read the passage on Photocopiable Sheet 7, ask the following questions.

Examples of questions at a literal level.

1. Which countries borrowed money?

2. Who did they borrow from?

3. Why can they not spend money on their own people?

4. What happens when they cannot pay back what they have borrowed?

5. Name three problems the poor countries have.

6. Why is it impossible for poor countries to get richer?

Level 2: The African Famine

If your pupil can answer the literal questions on Photocopiable Sheet 8, ask the following questions:

**Examples of questions at higher levels
(inferential and evaluative)**

1 Which of the following opinions do you think the author of this passage would agree with?

   a African people should organise themselves better so that they can cope better when the weather is bad.　*true/false*

   b The rich countries help the poorer countries in the best possible way.　*true/false*

   c It would be a benefit to the rich countries if the poor countries could buy more goods from them.　*true/false*

2 Find a word in the passage that means the same as 'organisations'. [Notice how well the reader can skim for the answer.]

3 Find a word in the passage that means the same as 'became aware'. [Notice how well the reader can skim for the answer.]

4 Why has the problem become worse?
   Is it because:
   ● There are too many wars?
   ● There are not enough roads?
   ● The population has grown?

5 Who do you suppose Bob is in the final paragraph?

Check comprehension and recall of Sheet 7 on a later occasion using Sheet 10.

Level 1: Second World War

Read the following passage and your teacher will tell you what to do.

In the Second World War the British _____ became healthier. Children from poor families were given meals at school and had milk, orange _____ and cod liver oil. There were more jobs for adults who were also given meals at work. People _____ less fat and sugar and only had meat once a week. Everyone could only buy _____ amounts of cheese, tea and eggs. Oranges and bananas, which came from abroad, were very hard to buy and so was chocolate. In 1942 ice cream _____ banned.

It was important to collect scrap metal, paper and wool. Children got medals for collecting _____ like old keys and books. People even gave the iron railings _____ their garden fences and the street outside their houses. The recycled metal was used to _____ planes. _____ was thrown away.

It was hard to buy new clothes. People had to wear second hand clothes. They mended anything they could. Some women painted a black line down the backs of their legs to look like they had _____ with seams on.

Food was grown everywhere. You could see vegetables growing on school _____ fields and in parks. Children went to the country to help with the harvest at the _____ of the summer. It was a good idea to have hens in your garden so you had your own supply of _____ .

Non-fiction Comprehension with Recall

Level 2: The African Famine

Read the following passage and your teacher will tell you what to do.

The African _____ have to borrow money from rich countries and from banks. Every year they have to pay more money _____ to the rich countries. They cannot spend money on their _____ people because they have to pay the rich countries. Often they cannot pay the rich countries, so they have to _____ more money. So things get worse. And _____.

There are other problems too. In some _____ of these countries there are no roads. There have been wars in Ethiopia, Sudan and Chad for many years. Governments spend _____ on the _____ things.

Aid _____ and the Ethiopian _____ knew that a famine was coming. They knew this in 1983, a year before the famine came. But the Ethiopian government seemed to do nothing. Nobody listened to the aid agencies, and the rich countries did _____.

In 1984 the rains did not come.

When people started _____, the television _____ arrived. The TV pictures shocked the world. When the world realised what was happening, aid _____ in to Ethiopia. But it was too _____ for many people. Thirty million people were _____ and one million died.

Cont'd

In 1985 there was plenty of _____. Farmers could grow _____ again. But there was still _____ answer to all the real problems. 1988 was another dry year and famine returned. A lot of aid givers realised that their money had not really _____ anything. It had helped people to stay _____ but the problems were still there. These problems will not go away until the rich countries _____ their ideas. The rich countries _____ many things from the poor countries, but they pay the _____ possible prices. Then the rich countries sell things to the poor countries at very _____ prices. So it is _____ for the poor countries to grow stronger and richer.

Aid is not used _____ enough. People are not always asked what _____ they need. So they get the wrong kind of help.

Aid must be given to the _____ people too. It must be given to the small farmers. In Africa, women do 80% of the farming work; but only 2% of aid _____ is given to women farmers.

Lastly, people from _____ countries must tell their governments to give more aid to the poorer _____ of the world. They should give more aid _____ the people in those countries need it. But it would also be good for the rich countries. If the poor countries were stronger and richer they could buy _____ things from the rich countries. That would be good for everybody. As Bob said to the European Parliament, 'You need Africa as much as they _____ you'.*

---

* Bob Geldof: The pop star who raised £70 million for famine relief in Ethiopia by Charlotte Gray, LDA edition written by D'Arcy Adrian-Vallance, Cambridge, 1989

Word Reading – Vocabulary Extension

3

Understanding single words is the starting point for full comprehension. Single word comprehension is linked to:

- decoding skills, i.e. the ability to sound out the word
- automatic word recognition, i.e. knowing immediately what the word is
- the reader's own spoken language, i.e. words he understands and uses.

Ideas for improving decoding skills and automatic word recognition of words are fully covered in *Target Reading Accuracy*. This chapter focuses on **increasing the size and flexibility of students' vocabularies**.

We learn new words in context and gradually refine their meanings. Children's 'preschool' vocabulary relates to everyday activities. At school, they have to learn abstract words, topic words and subject specific vocabulary. The meaning of a word can change according to the subject; consider 'bug' in Biology, ICT and Health Studies.

Two major aspects affect comprehension of single words:

1 Morphology (word structure)

Prefixes and suffixes added to a root word may alter its meaning or grammatical function.

Prefix – letter(s) added to the beginning of a word which change its meaning or function, e.g. *un*do, *a*float, *mis*take, *sub*standard.

> **Suffix** – letter(s) added to the end of a word to change its meaning or function, e.g. cross*ed*, duck*ling*, avail*able*, wedd*ings*.

Some words may have many possible prefixes and suffixes, e.g. **help**:

help**ed**   help**ful**   **un**helpful   help**fully**   **un**help**fully**

Once readers know how root words change they can understand more words.

2   Relationships between words

Words are organised and linked in many different ways:

- **synonyms** – words with very similar meanings
  e.g.   *little/small, help/assist, chuckle/giggle*

- **antonyms** – words with opposite meanings
  e.g.   *noisy/quiet, difficult/easy, strong/weak*

- **part/whole relationships**
  e.g.   *body – arm, leg, hand, head, neck*
         car – steering wheel, bonnet, windscreen

- **categories** – words which can be grouped
  e.g.   *flowers – rose, daffodil, tulip, daisy*
         transport – boat, ferry, plane, bicycle

- **pairs** – words which often go together
  e.g.   *uncle and aunt, salt and pepper, peaches and cream*

- **related words** – words we group by similarities
  e.g.   *tablecloth, napkin, towel* – all cloths used in the home
         rug, tablecloth, skirt – made of fabric
         saucepan, wooden spoon, whisk – all used in cooking

- **phonological similarity** – words with similar sound patterns

    e.g.   *mine, me, mouse* – start with the same sound, i.e. alliteration

    mine, fine, sign – rhyme

    office, table, booklet – each has two syllables.

ASSESSMENT

Formal

There may be useful information about the student's vocabulary in assessment reports, e.g.

- understanding of words (receptive vocabulary)
- ability to use words and define them (expressive vocabulary)
- speech and language processing difficulties.

Informal

Listen to the student in class.

Ask these questions:

- Does the student's vocabulary **sound** less mature than his/her peers?

- Does he use a narrow **range** of words?

- Does he use many clichés or 'stock phrases' (e.g. *at this moment in time, whatever, you know what I mean*)?

- Are non-specific words (e.g. *nice, like, get*) over-used?

- Does the student struggle to find words? This might be shown by hesitations, false starts, using descriptive phrases, mispronunciations, gestures or any difficulty in recalling the words he wants.

ACTIVITIES

Vocabulary-building activities are most effective when the words are those the student needs immediately. Choose words from topic or subject books. The student should be able to:

- see the word written and read it
- hear the word correctly pronounced and repeat it correctly
- understand the meaning(s) of the word
- retrieve the word and say it from a picture or written word
- practise the word in several different activities
- alter root words by adding prefixes and suffixes
- use the word in spoken phrases and sentences.

The type of activity depends on the vocabulary. Some words suit matching activities, others suit sorting activities. In all activities, encourage discussion. The more the word is used in different ways, the better.

Ideas for activities

Antonyms

Cut out antonyms and stick on plain cards. Shuffle the pack and ask students to pair them up.

Categories

- Decide a category and tell the students its name. Give them a pile of mixed words and ask them to choose those which fit the category.

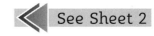

- As a more advanced exercise, ask them to order the groups.

example

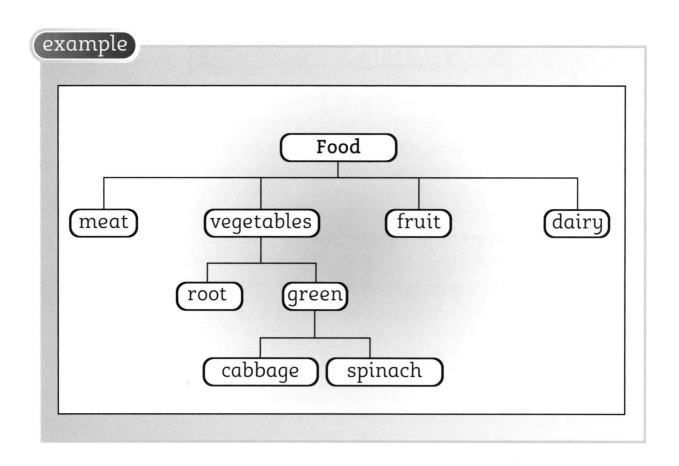

See Sheet 2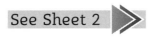

● Give several words in a category and include one which does not fit. Ask the student to tell you which is the odd one out and why:

   e.g.   rose tulip **carrot** daffodil geranium

See Sheet 2

● Give a category and ask for words in that category. This could be played as 'I went to market and I bought ...'.

See Target Card 1

Grading words

● Ask students to grade words:

   e.g.   cool – cold – chilly – freezing –
   fair – good – very good – excellent

Topic words

● Give a topic word and ask students to draw a word web.

42

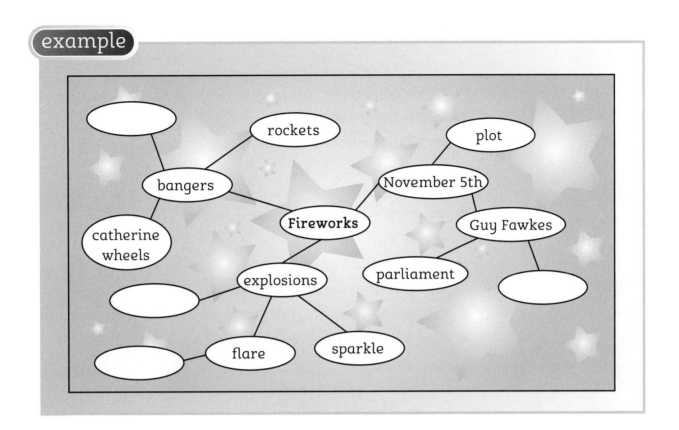

Synonyms

● Give students words and ask them to give two synonyms for each one.

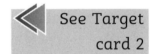

See Target card 2

Describing

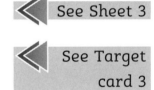

See Sheet 3

See Target card 3

● Ask students to think of adjectives. Link with the five senses. Ask them to collect as many words as they can for each sense to describe their home and environment.

Prefixes and suffixes

● Give a root word and ask for variations by adding prefixes and suffixes. Suggest a target number of words they can make.

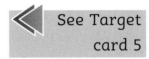

See Target card 5

Similarities and differences

Give a pair of words and ask for similarities and differences:

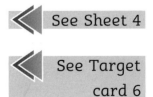

See Sheet 4

See Target card 6

    e.g.   a pair of jeans – school trousers

Similarities:

- long trousers
- have pockets
- worn by girls and boys
- can be washed in a washing machine

Differences:

- jeans are made of denim – school trousers of lightweight wool
- jeans are not allowed at school – school trousers are part of school uniform
- jeans are fashion clothing – school trousers are not
- jeans can be different styles – school trousers are the same.

Multi-meaning words

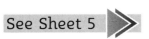

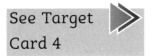

- Give multi-meaning words and ask students for different meanings.

Definitions

- Play a '20 Questions' quiz. Decide first whether answers have to be yes/no or whether open questions can be asked. Give one student a word. He should state if it is animal, vegetable or mineral (give help if needed). Tell others to ask questions until they guess the word.

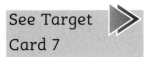

- Make a card game. Think of a word. Write clues to enable someone to guess it (or ask students to write clues). Put in a pack. The clue writer reads one clue at a time until the other student guesses the word.

  e.g.   clues for the word *navy*:
  - has two meanings
  - one is a colour
  - second includes ships at sea
  - rhymes with wavy

- the colour dark blue
- when men and women belong to this they wear uniform.

● Play a game in which one student covers an object or picture. He describes the object or picture one sentence at a time until the word is guessed.

Part/whole relationships

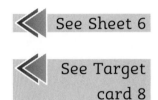

See Sheet 6

See Target card 8

● Give the students the *whole* word and ask them for the *parts*.

Resources

More ideas for activities can be found in:

1 *A Rainbow of Words – Activities to Promote Listening and Speaking* by Jeanne Holloway, published by NASEN

2 *The Language Parts Catalog – The World's Finest Selection of New and Improved Parts for Your Brain* by Dr. Mel Levine, published by Educators Publishing Service (obtainable from the Helen Arkell Dyslexia Centre)

3 *Reasoning and Reading (Levels 1 and 2)* by Joanne Carlisle, published by Educators Publishing Service Inc. (obtainable from the Helen Arkell Dyslexia Centre)

4 *Inclusion for Children with Speech and Language Impairments – Accessing the Curriculum and Promoting Personal and Social Development* by Kate Ripley, Jenny Barrett and Pam Fleming, published by David Fulton Publishers.

5 *Classi-Cards, Compa-Cards and Mastering Memory* from Communication and Learning Skills Centre, tel: 020 8642 4663, www.calsc.co.uk

Making or adapting games

Adapt commercial or homemade games and quizzes to make enjoyable activities for learning new words.

Play the following games using groups of words from the photocopiable sheets or topic words.

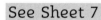

- **Race Game**: Make or adapt a race game (board game with numbered places). Make a pack of forfeit cards linked to your vocabulary aim, e.g. 'say five 2-syllable words' or 'say the opposite of black'.

  Players throw a die in turn. Each time a player lands on an even number he must 'pay a forfeit'.

- **Pelmanism/Pairs**: Make a pack of 15 pairs of cards. Customise them to target your teaching point. Mark the back of one of each pair with a star. Place cards face down. Each player selects a plain card and turns it face up. He then turns up one with a star and tries to make a pair. When a pair is made it is claimed. The winner is the player with most pairs.

See Sheet 1

- **Snap**: Make a set of 15 pairs of cards for Snap; this works well with synonyms, antonyms and pairs.

See Sheets 2 and 6

- **Happy Families**: Make 15 sets of four cards for Happy Families. This suits 'categories' or 'part/whole' relationships.

See Sheets 2, 3, 5 and 6

- **Bingo**: Make Bingo boards and matching cards. This game suits categories, whole/part relationships, multi-meaning words or collecting words for the senses.

Antonyms

tame	wild	agree	disagree
sweet	sour	beautiful	ugly
forget	remember	boring	interesting
open	closed	insult	compliment
dirty	clean	easy	difficult
strong	weak	heavy	light
cheerful	miserable	wide	narrow
after	before	first	last
start	finish	beginning	end
day	night	full	empty
straight	curved	right	wrong
asleep	awake	wet	dry
noisy	quiet	peace	war
large	small	dead	alive

furniture	games	boys' names
animals	colours	breakfast foods
parts of the body	clothes	cold things
vegetables	outdoor sports	hot drinks
sweets	cold drinks	musical instruments
girls' names	vehicles	round things
countries	counties	English/Scottish towns
magazines	authors	measurements
things in the sky	made of metal	made of wood
languages	flowers	dairy foods

Add extra categories of you own.

	Taste	
	Smell	
	Touch	
	Hearing	
	Sight	

jacket – sweater	sun – moon	bird – aeroplane
dress – skirt	boot – shoe	child – adult
wasp – fly	guitar – violin	clock – watch
deer – horse	basket – handbag	snow – rain
eye – ear	window – door	book – magazine

Multi-meaning Words

run	bug	long	class
trip	dear	can	ring
ball	links	book	turn
count	safe	draw	cross
right	fast	hand	play
light	rattle	stand	course
set	fix	scale	chord
port	form	shoot	mobile
down	miss	hold	bar
cool	break	bitter	bat
blow	jam	point	post
round	stamp	state	tip

Part/Whole Relationships

House:	wall	window	door	roof
Tree:	branch	roots	leaves	bark
Train:	carriage	engine	wheels	compartment
Car:	steering wheel	seats	engine	wheels
Book:	pages	chapters	cover	index

Can you think of 4 'parts' for each of the following 'wholes'?

Garden:

Castle:

Ship:

Aeroplane:

Supermarket:

Restaurant:

Cinema:

Kitchen:

Bathroom:

Race Game

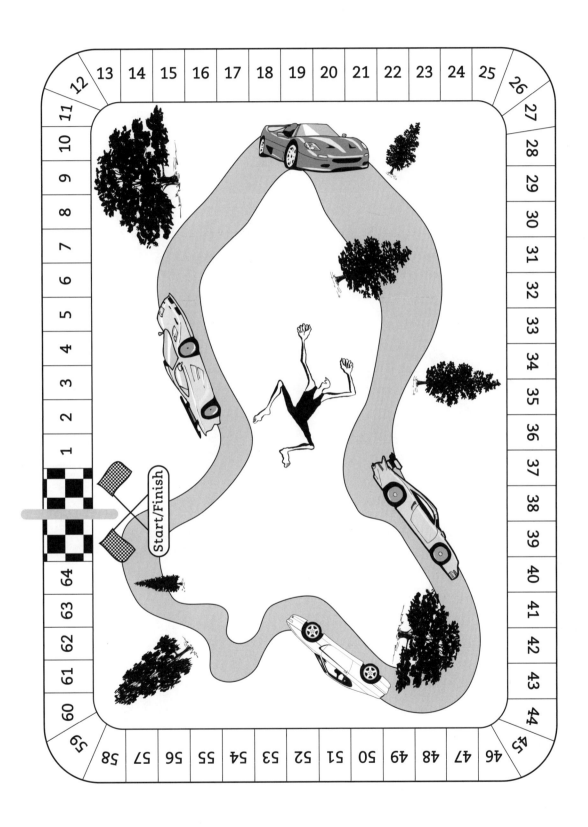

Aim: to give synonyms

Give 2 words similar in meaning,

e.g. tired: exhausted, weary.

big:

little:

hot:

bright:

Aim: to give two meanings

Give 2 sentences for each word to show 2 different meanings:

e.g. She kept cool by waving her fan.

He's a Manchester United fan.

order:

mixture:

hit:

hand:

mind:

Aim: to give words in a category

Give 5 words in each category,

e.g. **fish**: shark, tuna, mackerel, haddock, plaice.

musical instruments:

transport by air:

fizzy drinks:

counties:

Aim: to identify words according to each sense

Use Sheet 3.3 and sort these adjectives into the five senses. Add 2 each of your own to each sense,

e.g. buzzing – Hearing.

Taste / Sight / Touch / Smell / Hearing

huge – smelly – delicious – sticky – sweet – dazzling – smoky – tinkling – stinging – deafening – bright – stinking – salty – sunburnt – rough – musical – dark – crunchy – manky – yummy – clear – humming – sore – fresh - sour

Aim: to give similarities and differences

6

Give 3 similarities and 3 differences between these words,

e.g. house / flat
similarity: both homes
difference: house may be more than one floor, flat usually one floor.

ghost / fairy

horse / reindeer

beach / park

Aim: to make new words by adding prefixes and suffixes to a root word

5

Make as many new words as you can by adding prefixes or suffixes to these words,

e.g. sense: *sensible, nonsense, sensed, sensing.*

time:

honest:

wake:

please:

8

Aim: to give parts of a whole

Write 5 words which are part of each whole,

e.g. church: steeple, nave, choir, pew, font.

airport:

desert:

fairground:

jungle:

police station:

7

Aim: to give clues for a word

Give 5 clues for each word,

e.g. farm: in the country, has animals or fields, producing crops, rhymes with 'calm', etc.

wedding:

weather:

fireworks:

Sentences

4

Introduction

Many readers read and understand single words but have problems in comprehension when the words are put into sentences.

Some readers need to pay closer attention to meaning in order to understand. If they have to focus too hard on decoding, this will reduce their attention to meaning. These readers tend to be "plodders". Other readers are "skimmers" who pick up the gist and not always the accurate meaning.

Sentence structure can make it harder to understand. In a long sentence it may be difficult for the reader to 'hold on' to earlier parts which need to be processed later. This is a problem for those with working/short-term memory problems.

> **Short-term memory** – a temporary memory. Most people can hold at one time seven, plus or minus two, 'chunks' of information. Some poor readers have less short-term memory capacity than average readers.

Sentence structure can make it easier to understand. For instance, the sentence structure may make the meaning of a multi-meaning word clear, e.g. the horse had *flies* around its eyes, Jake had *flies* in his new jeans.

SENTENCE FEATURES AND ACTIVITIES

Read the following section on sentence features. Consider which of these affect your reader. Use the activities for any necessary practice with these features.

Alternatively, work through all the activities in order to boost students' ability to deal with these features.

Words in context

Sometimes the context enables readers to work out the meaning.

e.g. *Although he is only nine years old, his trumpet performance was* **superlative**.

It is clear that superlative means something like *high quality* or *excellent*.

Multi-meaning words

Some words have many meanings, e.g. **bug**. Does it make you think of insects, flu, problems with your computer ...?

Context can make meaning clear,

e.g. *The soldier wished to* **desert** *his regiment.*

The context tells us that **desert** means to **leave** and does not refer to a **sandy region**.

Some readers need help with understanding and using multi-meaning words flexibly. See Chapter 3 – 'Word Reading – Vocabulary Extension'.

Sentence length

If sentence length is excessive, it may make it hard to understand due to short-term memory problems. The reader may not remember the beginning of the sentence by the time he has come to the end. Too much effort put into decoding may not leave enough processing space for understanding. This is worse with embedded clauses.

See Sheet 1

See Target Card 1

e.g. *David Beckham, a famous footballer player, amazed his many fans, who had admired his football playing for a number of years, when he announced that he had a part in a new Hollywood film.*

Sentence structure

This may be simple or complex. If a sentence has many clauses, the reader may lose the sense.

A simple sentence will make one statement:
The man drove to the supermarket.

A simple sentence can be expanded into two statements by a conjunction.

> **example**
>
> Examples of **conjunctions** include:
>
> and, but, because, since, until, after, although, when, where, while, before.

Each statement has equal importance,

e.g. *The man drove to the supermarket* **and** *he bought some food.*
The man drove to the supermarket **but** *he did not buy anything.*

Sentences become more difficult if expanded with conjunctions which make one part of the sentence more important than the rest.

If a conjunction comes at the beginning of the sentence it can make it harder to understand,

e.g. **After** *he washed the car, he drove to the supermarket.*

Some readers find it difficult to know that the main idea in this sentence is '*He drove to the supermarket*'.

Passive sentences

> In a *passive sentence* the subject is not prominent, e.g. *The mouse was killed by the cat* instead of *The cat killed the mouse*. The cat is the subject, doing the action.

See Sheet 3

Readers may not understand passive sentences until they are around nine years old. A sentence such as:

Max, Marie-Lou and Joseph were pushed by the children from next door. (passive)

may be harder to understand than:

The children from next door pushed Max, Marie-Lou and Joseph. (active)

The best results in the end of term exams were those gained by Maxine and Hugh. (passive)

may be harder to understand than:

Maxine and Hugh gained the best results in the end of term exams. (active)

Cause–effect

Cause–effect sentences are hard because the order in which things happen is changed.

e.g. *He has a black eye* **because** *he walked into an open cupboard door.*

He walked into the door **first**, **then** he had a black eye.

Link words

'**Link**' words on their own do not have much meaning, but in context, and sometimes in pairs, they affect the meaning, e.g. *if, unless, if … then, all … except, either … or.*

e.g. **All** *the men washed their cars* **except** *the man who drove to the supermarket.*

Sometimes link words are similar but not identical. Readers need to give these close attention:

e.g. *Put the bread in the oven when it has risen.*
While the bread is rising put it in the oven.

In the first sentence the word **when** is important as it signifies that the bread must not be put into the oven **until** it has risen. In the second sentence the word **while** is important as it signifies that at any point during the time that the bread is rising, it can be put into the oven.

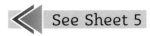
See Sheet 5

Phrase reading

If sentences can be read in phrases, meaning is easier to process,

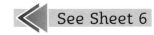
See Sheet 6

e.g. *They all lived / in a four bedroom house / just outside Cardiff.*

Fact/opinion

Some readers find it hard to distinguish fact from opinion.

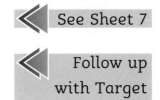
See Sheet 7

Follow up
with Target
Card 3

A fact is a statement which is always true,

e.g. *All circles are round.*

This is a **fact** because it is always true.

> *All English words have letters.*

This is a **fact** because it is always true.

> *Everyone likes ice-cream.*

This is not a fact. It is not true of everyone. Therefore it is an **opinion**.

Order of words

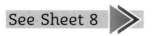See Sheet 8

The order of words in a sentence can radically change its meaning,

e.g. *The dancer who had dark hair spoke to the stranger.*

is different in meaning from:

The dancer spoke to the stranger who had dark hair.

Sometimes the meaning is less clear,

e.g. *The cat behind the door scratched the table leg.*

and

The cat scratched the table leg behind the door.

Do these sentences mean the same thing or could they have a different meaning?

Figurative language

> *Figurative language* is where the meaning is not literal.

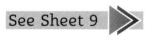See Sheet 9

English has much figurative language, which may not always be clear to readers. Phrases like *bright as a daisy* or *raining cats and dogs* need to be understood in context. Understanding figurative language develops in upper primary and secondary schooling. Some readers need help in understanding beyond the literal.

FOLLOW-ON ACTIVITIES

These follow-on activities provide further practice for reading at sentence level.

- **Silly Sentences** encourage the reader to give attention to precise meaning.

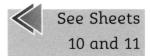 See Sheets 10 and 11

- **What's Missing?** Encourages the reader to check that he has the complete information.

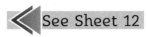 See Sheet 12

- **Yes/No/Maybe** and **Same or Different** encourage precise understanding.

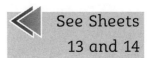 See Sheets 13 and 14

- **Sequencing Words in Sentences** encourages the reader to think of word order and how this affects meaning.

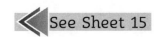 See Sheet 15

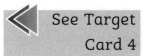 See Target Card 4

Words in Context

Read the following sentences and think about what the words in bold mean. The rest of the sentence should give you some clues. THINK!

1. In order to **increase** your examination marks you must do more work.

2. The angry customer was loud and **querulous** in making her complaints.

3. He could remain in the football club if he agreed to **demotion** to a lower team.

4. Spending a long period of time travelling around the world each year is **incompatible** with keeping up with family and friends at home.

5. He had a **morbid** interest in weapons, guns and death.

6. The criminal was given the maximum **penalty** of five years in prison.

7. I think he was perfectly **reasonable** to expect his guests to thank him for the party.

8. Nick was different from his generous brother; Nick was **parsimonious** when it came to buying Christmas presents.

Read the following sentences and underline the main idea.

Clue: the main idea is the part of the sentence that makes sense on its own.

1 He stayed at home so that he could watch the tennis.

2 The glass fell on the floor when the girl pulled at the tablecloth.

3 Before you clean your teeth take your medicine.

4 Long after the party was over the candles were still burning.

5 Right at the back of the vegetable garden I found the lawn mower.

6 Fred broke his leg when he was on a skiing holiday.

7 Once she had washed her hair Kim went out to the party.

8 All my friends like new trainers even though they are expensive.

9 The band ended their tour this week because they were worn out.

10 When EastEnders is over we will have supper.

Passive Sentences

Read the following sentences and answer the questions.

1 *The dish was broken by the new waitress.*
Who broke the dish?

2 *Lower income tax was announced by the Prime Minister.*
Who announced the lower income tax?

3 *The top selling CD was recorded by the winner of the pop contest.*
Who recorded the top selling CD?

4 *The swimmer was stung by a jelly fish.*
What stung the swimmer?

5 *The house was sold by the new estate agent in town.*
Who sold the house?

6 *The last goal was scored by David Beckham.*
Who scored the last goal?

7 *The garden was looked after by the man next door.*
Who looked after the garden?

8 *My computer game was bought by my grandma.*
Who bought the computer game?

9 *The best pizzas are sold by Pizza Palace.*
Who sells the best pizzas?

10 *The film was seen by many fans.*
Who saw the film?

11 *The children were chased by the bull.*
What chased the children?

12 *The letter was delivered by the postman.*
Who delivered the letter?

13 *The lorry was slowed down by the fog.*
What slowed the lorry down?

14 *The city was seen by many tourists.*
Who saw the city?

15 *The car was washed by the boys in the car park.*
Who washed the car?

Cause–Effect

Read the following sentences and underline the event which happened first.

1 The cat climbed up the tree because the dog was chasing him.

2 Because it had started to rain the woman put up her umbrella.

3 Because it had been a very hot summer there was a shortage of ice-cream.

4 The pupils started to fool around because they saw it was nearly break time.

5 The car braked suddenly because a child ran onto the street.

6 The footballers were furious because they thought the referee had been unfair.

7 Because they knew the roads would be busy they left early for the concert.

8 The computer was not working because there was a power failure.

Link Words

Read the following pairs of sentences. Discuss why they mean something different with your partner or teacher.

Pay special attention to the highlighted words.

1. Joe cannot go to the party **unless** his sister goes with him.
   Joe cannot go the party **if** his sister goes with him.

2. Maxine cannot go to school **if** she is ill.
   Maxine cannot go to school **until** she is ill.

3. **If** Lia turns up we will watch the video.
   When Lia turns up we will watch the video.

4. Robin will sleep **until** lunchtime **unless** someone drags him out of bed.
   Unless Robin sleeps **until** lunchtime, someone drags him out of bed.

5. **Neither** Eddy **nor** Henry was at home.
   Either Eddy **or** Henry was at home.

6. Razia likes to stay with her sister **if** her brother comes too.
   Razia likes to stay with her sister **unless** her brother comes too.

7. **Unless** Andy is at home they will have to take a taxi.
   If Andy is at home they will have to take a taxi.

8. Sophie can stay in the room **until** it is one o'clock.
   Sophie can stay in the room **because** it is one o'clock.

9. **If** Micky rings, tell him Kate is out.
   When Micky rings, tell him Kate is out.

10. Emily will go the party **only** with Megan.
    Only Emily will go to the party with Megan.

Phrase Reading

Mark the following sentences into phrases.

e.g. They made their way/to the shop/in the middle of the street.

1. Lia went to the swimming pool and after the first half-hour decided to spend most of her time practising diving. *(4 parts)*

2. Kate's music teacher was delighted when Kate won the top prize in the violin section of the competition. *(3 parts)*

3. Conal wanted to act in the school play but he knew that he had no time for rehearsals as his exams were starting very soon. *(3 parts)*

4. Elizabeth needed some cash so she looked for a holiday job at Tesco but she did not get one as she was not old enough. *(4 parts)*

5. The AK47 gun was fired again and again. *(2 parts)*

6. He stared at the long line of animals making their way across a muddy field. *(4 parts)*

7. She wore a black cloak and had a silver crown on her head. *(3 parts)*

8. Everyone looked up and saw thousands of bright stars twinkling in the sky. *(3 parts)*

9. He waved and a friend from school, called Dan, waved back. *(4 parts)*

10. They went on holiday to an island in the middle of the Pacific Island. *(3 parts)*

Fact/Opinion

Read the following sentences and circle whether they are fact or opinion.

1	All triangles have angles.	Fact/opinion
2	All apples are green.	Fact/opinion
3	Buses are more comfortable than trains.	Fact/opinion
4	There are four seasons in the year.	Fact/opinion
5	Newcastle United is the best football team.	Fact/opinion
6	Planes fly in the sky.	Fact/opinion
7	Girls are smarter than boys.	Fact/opinion
8	Brazil is in South America.	Fact/opinion
9	Flour is an ingredient of bread.	Fact/opinion
10	Art is the easiest subject at school.	Fact/opinion

Order of Words

● Do these pairs of sentences mean the same or not?

● If they are different, say the meaning of each sentence.

1. The man around the corner walked quickly.
   The man walked quickly around the corner.   Same/different

2. During the summer he goes sailing.
   He goes sailing during the summer.   Same/different

3. All the runners drank water during the race.
   The runners drank all the water during the race.   Same/different

4. Philip and Martin often go to the cinema together.
   Martin and Philip often go to the cinema together. Same/different

5. Some of the children went to the cinema on Sundays.
   The children went to the cinema on some of the
   Sundays.   Same/different

6. Ben left only his trainers at his friend's house.
   Ben left his trainers only at his friend's house only. Same/different

7. James lives across the street from his friend Lloyd.
   Lloyd lives across the street from his friend James. Same/different

8. Only Kim likes chocolate cake.
   Kim only likes chocolate cake.   Same/different

9. Unless we go out tonight we will have pizza.
   We will have pizza unless we go out tonight.   Same/different

Figurative Language

Read and discuss the meaning of the following phrases which are all examples of figurative language.

Figurative language is where the meaning is not literal, e.g. 'raining cats and dogs' means it is raining heavily.

- Hold your tongue
- Take the bull by the horns
- Jump on the bandwagon
- Keep an eye on something
- Pull your socks up
- Pull someone's leg
- All hands on deck
- Sell like hot cakes

- Kick the bucket
- Put on the back burner
- The buck stops here
- Let the cat out of the bag
- Get your skates on
- Hold your horses
- Eat humble pie
- Bright as a button

Silly Sentences

Encourage readers to spot the silly parts of sentences to promote deeper attention.

1 The cat went to the gate and ate his tail.

2 The dog has four legs and a wing on its back.

3 A kangaroo is in a saucepan and is playing with a baby kangaroo.

4 The coat is singing and is hanging on the hook.

5 The egg went for a walk after it was cooked.

6 The lorry had its supper and then drove to London.

7 The dish was white and hot and it broke the soup.

8 The bag had a zip with red lips.

9 The fish and chips had a dream.

10 The boy had a red balloon and it sang a silly song.

11 Dry your hands with the soap and then have your dinner.

12 She stuck some stickers on her book and then some paper clips on the roof.

Make the activity more challenging by interspersing silly sentences with sensible ones so that the reader has to be even more alert.

More Silly Sentences

Readers can formulate their own silly sentences by combining words from each of the following categories. This is an idea taken from 'Clear and Lively Writing' by Priscilla Vail.* She offers the following example, here slightly adapted from the original exercise called 'Elements'.

Put each of these words or phrases on blank cards and sort into the 'wh' categories.

Have the readers choose one phrase from each category and combine them to make a sentence. Read it aloud.

Ask the group to decide if it makes sense or not.

Who?

the alligator

Joe

the ballet dancer

the lion tamer

the carpenter

my teacher

your uncle

a policeman

my parents

the whole class

What?

ate a balloon

let off a firecracker

went on a trip

visited his brother

wrote a book

read a poem

sang a song

heard a horn

drove a nail

got a splinter

When?

today

yesterday

last year

this morning

at midnight

at dawn

at three o'clock

around suppertime

in 1845

on his birthday

Where?

up the chimney

in the supermarket

at the cinema

beside the door

over the roof

under the chair

everywhere

in the drawer

outside

in the kitchen

Cont'd

The sentences can be extended by adding this fifth category:

Why?

because it was cold

since he was late

because the dog left

because my father said so

because the room was too small

because the balloon popped

because I was laughing

because they were frightened

since we all wanted to

since it was a surprise

When the sentences have been combined, mix all the words up and get the students to put them back in their categories: Who? What? Where? When? Why?

Ask the students to make different sentences with one or two bits missing. The rest of the group should then ask appropriate questions using the 'wh' question words. This is a useful activity to help students to formulate questions about their reading in general.

---

* Vail, Priscilla L. *Clear and Lively Writing*. Walker and Company, New York. 0-8027-0682-7. Language games and activities for everyone.

Use the following sentences and ask your students to work out what information is missing.

1	Manchester United won it.
2	Trains run faster.
3	Can the taxi-driver take me there at five o'clock?
4	They are arriving tonight.
5	Call me before my next appointment.
6	I took his cap by mistake.
7	Collect my jacket from one of the dry-cleaners in town.
8	That boy was rude to me.

Yes/No/Maybe

The answer to each of these questions is **Yes**, **No** or **Maybe**

1   Lizzie won't wear her new jeans unless Maddy does.

     Will Lizzie wear her new jeans?   **Yes/No/Maybe**

2   Maybe the girls wouldn't have got wet if they had brought their umbrellas.

     Did the girls get wet?   **Yes/No/Maybe**

3   Rhona usually has pizza on Saturdays.

     Will Rhona have a pizza next Saturday?   **Yes/No/Maybe**

4   They think that John will pass his exam.

     Will John pass his exam?   **Yes/No/Maybe**

5   Charlie believes that his teacher is angry with him.

     Is Charlie's teacher pleased with him?   **Yes/No/Maybe**

Same or Different

Do these sentences mean the same as each other or are they different in meaning?

1. Most of the papers were read on their journey.

   A few of the papers were still not read after the journey.

   Same/Different

2. He took the only packet of biscuits left on the shelf.

   He only took the packet of biscuits on the shelf.   Same/Different

3. Every car has an engine.

   No car is without an engine.   Same/Different

4. Fred just went to the cinema.

   Only Fred went to the cinema.   Same/Different

5. Since Rose went away, the house is quieter.

   When Rose is at home the house is not as quiet.   Same/Different

6. Until the sun went down we walked along the beach.

   When the sun went down we walked along
   the beach.   Same/Different

Sequencing Words in Sentences

1 Copy the following sentences and cut up each sentence into individual words. Ask your students to arrange them into a sensible order.

What is your address?

Tom bought tickets for the London Eye.

Joe woke up with a sore throat.

2 Now do the same with these longer sentences.

The girl bought a bunch of red flowers.

She is going home after the party.

They were all late for school on Thursday.

The man was surprised when he won the lottery.

She is bad tempered because she is tired.

She is being bullied by the older girl.

The window was broken by Lee.

3 Cut the next sentence up into phrases.

The footballer was away for two weeks because he had been injured by another player in the first game of the season.

Find the key idea in sentences

Choose a text.

Find some long sentences. (You may need a helper to find these for you.)

In each sentence highlight the main idea.

Put a tick in the box each time you find the main idea.

☐☐☐☐☐☐☐☐☐
☐

Sequencing words in sentences

Do this with a partner.

Both of you must find a sentence from any text or newspaper.

Copy the sentence if necessary.

Cut it up into individual words.

Give your partner the words to rearrange.

If you are stuck, you can ask your partner for a little help.

Record how many words there are in your sentence.

Next time go for an even longer sentence.

Reading for meaning

Guess what the word means even if you have not read it before.

This is not all guesswork. You are a detective at work. Use clues you pick up from the rest of the sentence or text.

Read some text and highlight any words that you do not understand.

Have a go at working out what they mean.

Check with a helper.

Put a tick in the box each time you work out a new word.

☐☐☐☐☐☐☐☐

Fact/opinion

Sometimes writers make opinions seem like facts. We see many examples of this in advertising.

Look at some magazines and find examples of where the writer tries to convince us that something is a fact. Advertisements are the best place to look.

Find five examples and either highlight them or copy them to show the class or group.

Put a tick in the box each time you find an opinion that sounds like a fact.

☐☐☐☐☐

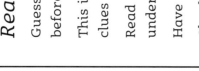

Paragraphs and Longer Texts

Paragraphs have a **unity** of topic or take events forward in a particular sense. Different types of paragraphs may show different kinds of structure, such as:

- time order or a sequence of events in narrative
- cause–effect
- similarities and differences
- sequential information for instructions or procedures
- explanatory, factual or descriptive.

Readers need to:

- spot topic sentences
- extract key ideas
- detect structure
- work out inferences
- be evaluative and critical in their response to longer texts.

Paragraphs in factual texts often have **topic** sentences which state the main points and supporting sentences which give the details. Link words or phrases make connections within the paragraph or with adjoining paragraphs.

Unity of the paragraph

 See Sheet 1

Tip: use information downloaded from the Internet.

One good way to demonstrate to readers that a paragraph should have unity is to introduce them to paragraphs with irrelevant sentences hidden in them.

Take paragraphs from any texts and add irrelevant sentences.

Topic sentences

 See Sheet 2

The **topic sentence** gives the overall sense and often comes at the beginning or end of the paragraph. Where there is no topic sentence, good readers will be able to sum up the sense but poor readers may not.

See Sheet 12

Give paragraphs where there is a clear topic sentence and ask the reader to identify it. Good textbooks at Key Stages 2 and 3 provide plenty of examples. Look at the paragraph on Sheet 12 – 'Limestone Caves'. The first sentence is the topic sentence.

Work first with simple narrative and information paragraphs. Write the following passage on the board:

Direct your students to:

- find **topic sentences** and key ideas
- find **supporting details** for topic sentences.

The **topic sentence** is: *You can do all sorts of things on your summer holidays.*

You can do all sorts of things on your summer holidays. You can relax at home or go away. You can go on an activity holiday or lie on the beach and sunbathe. As long as you have your friends with you, you know you will enjoy yourself.

Supporting details are:

- relax at home
- activity holiday
- go away
- relax on the beach.

Some paragraphs have a concluding sentence to round them off. Here we have *"As long as you have your friends with you, you know you will enjoy yourself"*.

Main idea

After working on topic sentences, ask readers to identify the main idea of different passages.

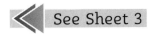 See Sheet 3

Sequence of information

Encourage the reader to appreciate that the order in which information appears in a paragraph is important.

- If readers have difficulty with the logical sequence, read the sentences and highlight the signpost words, which indicate the order.

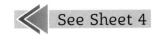 See Sheet 4

- Start with a complete sentence which does not need anything to come before it.

- If necessary, use arrows to draw connections.

For more advanced readers use harder paragraphs:

- Copy each paragraph and enlarge if possible.

- Cut each paragraph into separate sentences.

- Mix up the sentences in each paragraph.

- Ask students to put them in the correct sequence.

- Ask them to highlight the link words.

Signpost words

See Sheet 5
Provide many examples of different kinds of signpost words. They guide the reader through longer texts.

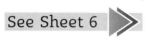
See Sheet 6
Give examples of passages that can be used for finding signpost words.

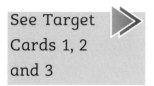
See Target Cards 1, 2 and 3
Target Cards 1 and 2 should be given to students who need this kind of training. When they are more proficient move to Target Card 3.

More complex structures

Cause–Effect

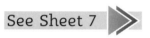
See Sheet 7

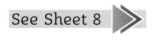
See also section on cause–effect sentences in Chapter 4, Sheet 4
Ask students to read the paragraph on Sheet 7 and answer the questions in order to work out the reasons why things happened.

Similarities and differences

Some paragraphs are structured by comparing two or more things. (This is an extension of the work on similarities and differences at word level in Chapter 3.)

See Sheet 8
Ask students to read the paragraph on Sheet 8. Ask them to name all the similarities and differences between pizzas and beefburgers.

Inferences

Inferences are when we make conclusions from evidence we see. If we arrive home to an empty house and see the front door wide open, we may conclude that we have had a burglary.

The same thing happens when we read, but some readers find it difficult to read between the lines. Making inferences is picking up clues in the text and drawing conclusions,

e.g. *The leaves were turning brown and the evenings were growing shorter. There was a sudden chill in the air.*
    The reader may conclude that it is autumn.

Ask students to read Sheets 9 and 10 and answer the questions.

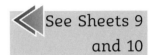

See Sheets 9 and 10

This kind of activity can be extended for more capable students by encouraging them to think of other, less obvious explanations,

e.g. *The lady looked horrified when she looked in the mirror because it was dirty and cracked.*

    All the cars slowed down because a cow was wandering across the motorway, because a new aeroplane was flying overhead, etc.

One way of developing inferential skills in pupils is to demonstrate the different kinds of comprehension questions. There are:

- questions that have answers clearly on the page
- questions that you have to think about.

Write the text below on the board and use for discussion:

> That night he called his sister in New York. He was anxious about talking to her and telling her about his father's visit to the doctor.

Questions that have answers on the page:

- When did he make the phone call?
- Who did he call?
- Where was the person who was receiving the phone call?

Questions you have to think about:

- Did his sister live in the United States?
  Yes. You have to know that New York is in the United States.

- Do you think his father is well?
  No, because he is worried about telling his sister about his father's visit to the doctor, which probably means his father is unwell.

For further activities see *New Thinking and Reading, Levels 1-6, Exercises in Inferential Comprehension*, published by Learning Materials Ltd.

See Target Card 4

Students may need the following **prompts** for designing questions whose answers do not appear on the page, i.e. answers they need to think about. These questions can begin with:

- **Who** do you **think** ...?
- **What** do you **think** ...?
- **How** do you **think** ...?
- **When** do you **think** ...?
- **Where** do you **think** ...?
- **Why** do you **think** ...?

Understanding of factual information

See Sheets 11, 12, 13 and 14

Encouraging the reader to demonstrate understanding by turning the text into a different format.

This prepares the way for the kind of work involved in Chapter 8 – 'Interactive Reading'.

Interpretation of the text

More advanced readers need practice in **reading beyond the text** and **understanding higher levels of meaning**.

Sheet 15 is an example of the highest form of comprehension practice. The earlier stages are: decoding with ease, and literal comprehension at word, sentence and paragraph level.

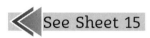See Sheet 15

- Read the passage and discuss what this story means. This can be carried out as a group or class activity.

- Remind the group that there is not one right answer.

- We all bring different knowledge and understanding of the world to the reading process.

- The discussion can centre around:
  - the lesson that the old woman was being taught
  - whether the group think she has learned the lesson
  - what is happiness.

This exercise prepares the reader for the highest stage of reading, where the reader needs to interpret the author's intention.

Irrelevant Sentences

Read the paragraphs below and spot the sentences that do not fit in each one.

1. In 1912 the *Titanic* made its first voyage. People thought it was unsinkable. It was the largest ocean liner in the world and it was like a top class hotel. Before the end of the voyage an iceberg hit it. This was two years before the first world war. The ship sank in only 3 hours. More than 1500 people died. This was the world's most famous shipwreck. You can see the story of the shipwreck in the film called *Titanic*.

3. Cosmetics were invented thousands of years ago. Men and women wore make-up in Ancient Egypt. The make-up was not to make them look good. It was to protect their skin from the sun and insects. They used soot in the paint they put on their eyes. Nowadays you can go to Egypt for a holiday.

3. The Manning Gallery is marking the centenary of the birth of the famous artist, John Fiddler. August is a busy month for exhibitions. They are putting on a major exhibition of his most well-known landscapes. There will be paintings, watercolours and photographs mainly from his work in the south of England.

4. The Fox Inn is an excellent place to stay if you are travelling to Cornwall. It was a coaching inn in the 18th century. The owners have decorated it to look like the original inn. Mrs Smith stayed in Wales last summer. It has eight bedrooms all with four-poster beds. There is a beautiful restaurant in the gallery. There are open fireplaces in all of the main reception rooms.

Topic Sentences

Underline the topic sentence in the following two paragraphs.

History topic

1 The reeve ran things for the lord. He said what to plant and when. He organised work like harvesting, which involved the whole village. He hired extra people at busy times. He sold spare crops, ran the lord's own land and made sure everyone did their jobs. If the strips of land the villeins farmed were changed, he decided who got which strips.*

Geography topic

2 Migration is the movement of people from one place to another. People move from their home for two reasons. Some feel that they can live a better life in another place. Others fear for their lives if they stay in their home, so they move away from the danger. Animals and birds also migrate. They migrate each year at different seasons.**

* Kelly, N., Rees, R. and Shuter, J., *Living through History Book 1: Roman Empire and Medieval Realms*. Heinemann
** Bateman, D. (1996) *The Oxford Children's A to Z of Geography*. Oxford University Press

Main Idea

Match the paragraphs to these titles.

A Trees at different times of the year
B Trees growing
C Looking for trees
D Trees are useful

1 You may be surprised to find that the best place to see trees is not the countryside, but in towns and cities. You'll find hundreds of different kinds of trees, often from other countries, in parks and gardens. They have been planted for their colourful flowers and leaves.

2 You may already know about some of the things we get from trees – wood, paper and maple syrup. But did you know we also get rubber and cork. Perhaps the best thing is something we cannot see – oxygen. Every growing tree pumps life-saving oxygen into the air and removes carbon dioxide. Too much carbon dioxide can make the Earth too warm.

3 In some parts of the world, there is a huge difference between the seasons of summer and winter, or between the dry season and the rainy season. Trees have to adapt to the changing seasons as best they can. Some lose all their leaves in the winter or in the dry season, while others just shed some of their leaves.

4 Twigs stick out from trees like thousands of tiny fingers. They are the growing end of the tree. Each twig has some buds which contain new shoots. When the time is right, these buds open. The shoots lengthen and then become new twigs. Buds also contain new leaves and flowers.*

* Gamlin, Linda, *Trees*. Dorling Kindersley. ISBN 0-7513-6000-7

Sequence of Information

Put the following sentences into a logical sequence.

Cut the passage into strips to help you move the sentences around.

It came off with no bother at all.

Then he went on up to his classroom.

He was always late.

It was late.

Roddy smiled and put the screwdriver back into his pocket.

It was a short, strong screwdriver, just the right size to fit into his pocket.

He tried it on a hook in the cloakroom.

Roddy found the screwdriver by the school gate.

Prince, Alison, *Screwloose*. 4U2read.ok. Barrington Stoke

Signpost Words

When you are reading, watch out for **signpost words**. These are words or phrases which are signposts to the meaning and structure of the text. They tell us how ideas are organised.

1 **Listing:**

firstly	thirdly	in the first place
next	secondly	last, finally

2 **Place and position:**

under	behind	above
on top of	inside	downwards

3 **Cause and effect:**

so	because	therefore
since	thus	

4 **Examples:**

for instance	one example is	for example
an illustration of this is		

5 **To introduce a different idea:**

but	and yet	nevertheless
although	on the other hand	

6 **To sum up:**

to summarise	it amounts to this	in other words
in conclusion		

7 **Time:**

then	previously	next
while	after that	when

8 **Importance:**

It is worth noting	It is vitally important that
A significant point is	The main focus is

9 **Rephrase:**

in other words	to put it another way
let me put it this way	that is to say

Highlight Signpost Words

Read the following passage and highlight any signpost words you can find.

The King of Spain decided not to visit Holland. While home events may have made it difficult for him to go at that time, it is worth noting that he knew he would never have a better chance to go. Secondly, the delay meant that Spain lost control of Holland. Thirdly, it was very expensive to keep such a big army. Because of this the King of Spain decided that Holland must pay the cost. So Holland agreed to have a new tax. Two years later the new tax had not been paid.

Read the following paragraph and answer the questions below.

Mum was not feeling well. She decided that she was too ill to go to the shops. She asked Johnny to go and get some tea, milk and biscuits from the shop at the end of the road and she gave him some money. When Johnny was walking down the road he met his friend Sam. They talked about last night's football game and then what they were going to do at the weekend. They did not notice time passing and suddenly Johnny realised that the shop would be closed. He went home and told his mother that he had been too late for the shops. She was very cross. She was even crosser when he found out that the money had gone from his pocket. And she was even crosser when some friends called round and there was no tea or biscuits.

1 Why didn't Mum go to the shops?

2 Why did Johnny go to the shop?

3 Why was the shop closed?

4 Why was Mum cross?

5 Why did she get even crosser?

Read the following paragraph.

Pizzas and beefburgers are both examples of fast food. They are both good value for money and easy to find. If you do not eat meat, you will not want a beefburger and if you are allergic to wheat, you cannot have a pizza. They both really fill you up if you are hungry and they go well with tomato ketchup. More grown-ups prefer pizza.

1　How is a pizza **like** a beefburger?

2　What are all the **differences** between pizzas and beefburgers?

What Inference Can You Make?

Read the following and answer the questions:

1 The waiter sighed when he saw his tip.

Why do you think he sighed?

2 The lady looked horrified when the hairdresser held up the mirror.

Why do you think she looked horrified?

3 The fat man loosened his belt after his dinner.

Why do you think he loosened his belt?

4 There was confetti all over the church car park.

Why do you think there was confetti all over the church car park?

5 All the cars have slowed down on the motorway.

Why do you think the cars have slowed down?

6 The student smiled when he opened the envelope with his exam results.

Why did he smile?

Which is the Best Inference?

Read the following and answer the questions.

1 Joe was tired and he was hot and sweaty. He was glad to arrive home and have a shower.

Which is the best inference to make?
- Joe had been to school.
- Joe had been in the gym.
- Joe was planning to do his homework.

2 Mum and Dad bought their tickets while Alex and Jan queued up for some popcorn.

Which is the best inference to make?
- The tickets were expensive.
- Alex and Jan had not had their supper.
- They were all going to the cinema.

3 Emily's head was aching. She kept blowing her nose and her eyes were watering.

Which is the best inference to make?
- Emily has the flu.
- Emily did not go to bed last night.
- Emily was going to make breakfast.

4 The boys were excited that they were going on a bike trip. They got up early and looked outside. They were very disappointed.

Which is the best inference to make?
- It was a lovely sunny day.
- It was raining.
- They saw their mother hanging out washing.

Emperor Penguins

Make a diagram or picture to show the information in the paragraph below.

Emperor penguins are the largest of all seabirds – length 112 cm, weight 20–40 kg. They live in the Antarctic. They live in large groups. They cannot fly, but are very good swimmers. They eat fish, squid and shrimps and have a very sharp bill. They live on pack ice. The birds feed several times a day, but during the breeding season the male can go without food for up to 115 days.

Limestone Caves

Read the following paragraph and draw a diagram to show the information.

Limestone caves contain beautiful features called stalactites and stalagmites. These form when water drips from the roofs of caves. Each drip deposits a tiny amount of calcium carbonate. Over hundreds and thousands of years the calcium carbonate builds up to form icicle-shaped columns. Columns hanging from the roof are called stalactites. Columns built up from the floor are called stalagmites. If stalactites and stalagmites meet they will form a column.**

River Basins

Read the following paragraph and draw a diagram to show the information.

Rivers begin in upland areas. The place where they begin is called the source. Rivers flow downhill from their source, until they reach the sea or a lake. The place where the river enters the sea or lake is called a mouth. During the journey from source to mouth the main river is joined by other rivers. This means a river can have several sources. The name given to a smaller river joining the main river is a tributary. The point where a tributary joins the river is called a confluence. When more water enters the river from a tributary, the river channel becomes wider and deeper. This means a river becomes larger as it flows from its source to its mouth.*

The Family of Planets

Read the following paragraph. Draw a picture which shows the positions of the planets in relationship to the Sun.

The shape of the solar system is like a plate. The Sun is in the centre, and the planets whizz around it (this is called being in orbit around the Sun). They are prevented from shooting off into space by the force of the Sun's gravity. Four planets are quite close to the Sun. First comes Mercury, then Venus, followed by Earth, then Mars. Further out are Jupiter and then Saturn. Then, after a big gap comes Uranus, followed by Neptune. Pluto is the farthest out, on the edge of the solar system.**

---

* Arnell, Adam, *Geography Key Stage 3*, pages 101–7. Letts Educational
** Adapted from Langley, A. (2000) *First Book of Space*. Oxford University Press

Once there was an old woman who lived in a vinegar bottle. It was rather a small bottle, and the old woman spent much of her time polishing the glass walls. This made her very grumpy.

"Oh dear" she would say, "what a terrible life I lead, living in this bottle, where everyone can see me. I wish I could live in a cottage with a little garden, and lace curtains at the window. I would be happy then!"

One day as she was saying these things to herself, an angel flew by and heard the old woman's words. The angel felt sorry for her, and in a flash the vinegar bottle was turned into a little cottage, with lace curtains at the window and a pretty garden. The old lady looked around her in wonder. Gone were the glass walls. She now had everything she wished. The angel smiled and went on its way.

Some time later the angel flew past the old woman's cottage, and heard a familiar sound.

"Oh dear, what a terrible life this is. Just a poky little cottage, a tiny garden and no room in which to put anything. I wish I had a proper house, with an upstairs, a nice big garden and a spare bedroom to put all my things in. Then I'd be happy!"

The angel heard the old woman's words, and was sorry that she was not happy. In a flash the cottage was transformed into a large house on two floors, with a long garden at the back. The old lady looked pleased. The angel smiled and went on its way.

Not long afterwards the angel came that way again, and heard a voice that it recognised.

Cont'd

"Oh dear, what a terrible life this is. A huge house and only me to look after it. All those stairs to go up and down, all those rooms to clean. A large garden to look after and no one to help me. I wish I could live in a palace, with servants to look after me, lovely clothes to wear and people to visit me. How happy I'd be then!"

The angel sighed when it heard the woman's words. In a flash the house was replaced by a great palace, with crystal chandeliers, and servants in every room. There were lovely gardens full of flowers and gardeners to look after them. There were cupboards full of dresses to wear, and many different bedrooms to choose from. The kitchens provided any food she wanted. All who saw this wonderful palace wanted to meet the lucky person who lived there. The old lady blinked in wonder. The angel smiled and went on its way.

Some time later the angel passed by the palace, and heard ...

"Oh dear, what a terrible life this is. So many people to see, so many servants to look after. Such a long way to walk, so many rooms and corridors. So much food it is making me fat, so many flowers I don't know what to do with, so many doors to open and close. What a life!"

Before she could say another word an amazing thing happened. In a flash of light the old woman found herself back in the vinegar bottle. And for all I know she is still there today.*

---

* 'European Folktale' (1996) in R. Fisher (ed.) *Stories for Thinking*. Nash Pollock Publishing

Identifying time signpost words

1 Find a book with a story.

2 Read the first paragraph or page.

3 Spot how many **time** words you can find.

4 The kind of words to look for are a time or date, like:

midnight, Sunday, September, 1988, noon, last week

then, when, before, later, soon, afterwards, the next day

Identifying place or position signpost words

1 Find a book with a story.

2 Read the first paragraph or page.

3 Spot how many **place or position** words you can find. These are words which tell you **where** something is.

4 The kind of words to look for are:

on top of, underneath, beside, over, outside, towards, beside, above, further away

Recognising all kinds of signpost words

1 Find a piece of writing from a textbook.

2 Read a paragraph or a page.

3 Spot how many **signal/link** words you can find.

4 Use Sheet 5 to help you.

If it is at the right reading level, you can use the story 'The Old Lady in the Vinegar Bottle' to do Target Cards 1, 2 and 3.

Distinguishing literal and inferential comprehension

Read a passage that your teacher has given to you.

Make up two or three questions that you can ask a partner to answer from just looking at the passage.

These questions can begin with the words:
WHO WHAT HOW WHEN WHERE WHY

Make up two or three questions that your partner needs to think about, where he cannot find the answer on the page.

Listening to Reading

- There are different ways of listening to reading, depending on the kind and degree of support offered.

- All of the following types of reading involve the reader and another person. Who can provide this kind of support? That depends on the activity involved.

- We need to listen to readers reading aloud to determine their accuracy in decoding. Poor and reluctant readers can find this stressful and difficult.

- Avoid asking these readers to read aloud in front of their peers.

- Reading aloud in a safe place such as with a parent or a teaching assistant can be less daunting.

Kind of reading	Who can help?
1 Paired reading	Following simple guidelines, anyone who can read can do this: **parent, classroom assistant** or **another student**.
2 Shared reading	Following simple guidelines, anyone who can read can do this: **parent, classroom assistant** or **another student**.
3 Prepared reading	This requires more skills and will probably need a trained **teacher** or a **classroom assistant**.
4 Pause, praise, prompt	This can be used effectively by a trained **parent, classroom assistant** or **student**.

1 Paired reading

Paired reading is where:

- the student reads to a helper, and
- the helper reads to the student, and
- sometimes they read together.
- The reader decides who reads and when, by giving a pre-arranged signal, such as tapping a pencil.

Paired reading is successful when:

- the reader chooses the text (interest heightens motivation and feeling of 'ownership')
- the activity is regular – little and often
- there are no strict rules
- there is a sensible routine for the individual reader
- the system is made as flexible as necessary.

For example:

- the helper reads everything first
- the helper reads again, with the student taking part as appropriate
- the student then reads alone with the helper supplying any word not instantly recognised
- this final stage is repeated as often as the reader wishes.

The reading is kept as fluent as possible and words unknown or stumbled over by the reader are supplied promptly by the helper.

2 Shared reading

If the helper is doing most of the reading, encourage the reader to follow the text and guess safe words. Use regular questions, such as asking what might happen next, to keep the reader focused.

Echo reading is a kind of paired reading. The helper reads aloud and the reader echoes what he hears about a second later, running a finger under the text as it is read.

Advantages of shared reading and paired reading:

- student chooses book
- flexibility
- no sense of failure – plenty of praise
- emphasis on understanding words
- example of expression and right pacing
- models of pronunciation of difficult words
- attention from helper
- increases amount of time for practice
- encourages comprehension.

3 Prepared reading

The aim of prepared reading is to facilitate easier decoding of the text and comprehension.

> **Decoding** – turning the written words into their spoken equivalents.

Preparation for decoding

See *Target Reading Accuracy* for ideas on preparing individual words for decoding.

Preparation for comprehension

- Introduce any specialised vocabulary.
- Discuss content.
- Provide questions for the reader to ask himself.
- Encourage the reader to think about what the text is going to contain.

- Skim through reading material, look at illustrations, diagrams, etc.
- If the book has been started, review the story line or topic so far.

For longer texts, consider listening to stories on tape, watching video versions or dramatisations, or having a helper read some or all of the text.

4 Pause, praise, prompt

This is a non-threatening technique to use.

Praise	for correct reading for self-correction for correction after a prompt
Pause	to give the student a chance to work out an unknown word
Prompt	If mistakes do not make sense, ask questions about the meaning. If mistakes do make sense, encourage the reader to look at the word: • what does the word begin with? • are there any smaller words in it? • can he sound it out and blend it together? If no response, ask the reader to read to the end of the sentence, or re-read the beginning and guess. After a couple of prompts, supply the word.

Reading to students

Reading to students has many advantages. It:

- gives practice in listening and concentration
- models fluency, expression and intonation
- extends vocabulary, imagination and knowledge of the world
- develops a sense of sequence and anticipation
- allows access to greater amount of literature
- can build a bond between reader and students.

More ideas ...

Here are some additional ideas for preparing for reading and encouraging comprehension of a narrative text.

Introducing a new book

- Look at the book cover. What does it tell you? What does it make you think?

- Consider concepts of print.

- directionality of words from left to right and moving from one line to the next

- orientation of letters which are easily confused, e.g. *b/d, u/n, m/w, t/f, p/q*

- the same letter in different forms, e.g. a, A, a, **A**

- sequence of letters and words, e.g. *on/no, saw/was, the dog bit the man/the man bit the dog*

- letter/sound links, e.g. *c = /k/ or /s/, ea* as in *seat, break, bread.*

- Discuss story line, characters and illustrations.

- Draw on what they already know and have experienced.

- Introduce and discuss new or unfamiliar words.

Questioning before, during or after reading

- Setting – where does the story take place? Is it a familiar setting to you?

- Characters – who are the main people? Who did you like, not like, or who interested you etc?

- Plot – what happened in the story and in what order did events take place?

- Feelings – how do you think particular characters felt? Can you identify with their feelings?

- Inferential comprehension – what did a character actually mean when he said ...?

- Prediction – what do you think might happen next and why?

NB If the reader is having difficulty, model good answers.

Types of Reading

Readers need to master basic decoding skills and develop sufficient fluency to let them understand text easily. Then they can move on to using different methods of reading. Many texts do not have to be read word by word. Readers need to decide why they are reading. Then they can decide how best to tackle a text.

Four questions will cover most educational purposes for reading. Tell the student to ask these questions before reading:

Do I want:	Strategy needed
1 a general idea of the text?	**Skimming** text
2 a specific piece of information?	**Scanning** text for key words or symbols
3 to understand the exact meaning?	**Accurate reading** of every word
4 to learn and remember this?	**Interactive reading** (see Chapter 8) for in-depth knowledge and understanding and full recall

This table is reproduced at the end of the chapter as Sheet 1.

Teach these four methods separately. Give readers opportunities first to practise each one, then to decide which one to use in any given reading task.

ASSESSMENT

Assess whether readers use these methods. Follow each activity by a discussion of individual approaches. Discuss what worked well and what did not.

1. **Skimming**: Tell students they will have thirty seconds to look at a page of text or a newspaper article. After thirty seconds tell them to turn it face down. Ask what they have found out. Then ask them **how** they found out that information. What did they **actually look at** on the page?

2. **Scanning**: Choose a page from a factual text or directory on which there are items of information identifiable by features such as numbers, symbols, capital letters or length of word. Ask students to find one piece of information as quickly as possible. Once they find it, ask **how** they did it. What **visual features** did they look for?

3. **Accurate reading**: Ask students to read a set of instructions; tell them they will have plenty of time and must be confident by the end that they can follow them accurately. When they have read the instructions, ask the students to describe in their own words exactly what they have to do. Press for absolute clarity. Ask them to think about **how** they did the reading task.

4. **Interactive reading**: Give students a piece of text to read and tell them that they will be asked to demonstrate their full understanding and knowledge of the contents. Then ask students to summarise or answer questions that probe their knowledge, understanding and recall. Then discuss **how** each student tackled the task.

Remember, when students are learning any new technique the reading material itself should be simple. This is not the time for new vocabulary and complex language structure. When techniques are 'second nature', students can apply them to harder material.

ACTIVITIES

1 Skimming

Students should understand that this is not just glancing through material. It needs focus and concentration to find out enough key information quickly. Give students timed activities to help them speed up. After each practice discuss how much each student has learned.

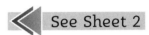
See Sheet 2

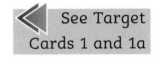
See Target Cards 1 and 1a

During the *skimming process* direct students to look at:

- title
- diagrams and charts
- captions
- first and last sentence
- any pictures or illustrations
- bold type
- any large print
- first and last paragraph.

If *skimming a whole book* to see if it contains the information required, this list might be modified:

- title
- chapter headings
- any brief summaries available
- table of contents
- introduction
- any chapter which looks particularly promising – using the list above.

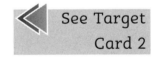
See Target Card 2

Advanced students can learn to *skim paragraphs* for the gist, i.e. only reading some words. This can be useful when deciding if a paragraph contains sufficient information to warrant thorough reading. To show that reasonable understanding is possible with words left out, take a piece of text and blot out all the words except the main content words, leave only the main nouns and verbs.

> ### example
>
> ... snails ... shell ... hide ... protect ... slugs ...
> slimy ... hard ... birds ... pick up.

Ask how much the reader has learned with this amount of information. Encourage practice of this basic *'speed reading'* with a complete text.

- Read the whole of the first sentence.

- Then let the eyes run along each line of text, skimming the main words. (Moving the finger rapidly under the lines may help.)

See Target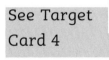
Card 3

- Finally, read the whole of the last sentence.

- How much do you know now?

2 Scanning

Scanning is looking at text for one piece of information or one detail only, such as a date, name or key word. This is how we find words in dictionaries or names in telephone books.

See Sheet 3 ▷▷

Give the students the book or piece of text and the word they need to find. First encourage them to *think* what it will look like!

See Target ▷▷
Card 4

- Is it likely to be long or short?
- Will it start with a capital letter?
- What is the first letter likely to be?
- Will there be a pattern in the letters?
- Will there be any numbers?

Then encourage them to 'visualise' what they know and scan with that in mind, not allowing their eyes to dwell on other distractions. The rest of the text should appear quite vague and hazy.

If a student is looking for a fact, encourage him to think of words it is likely to be near, as well as what form it will take.

3 Accurate reading

Sometimes every word counts! Ask the class for different examples of times when this is important to highlight the need for this type of reading. Encourage thinking about the full range of reading so that students understand how useful this method is in everyday life as well as at school, e.g.

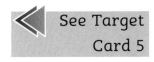
See Target
Card 5

- medicine bottle
- safety guidelines
- maths problem
- washing instructions for a new sweater
- instructions to build a model
- weedkiller can
- recipe ingredients
- homework instructions
- exam instructions
- directions to a friend's house

These tasks require careful and accurate reading.

Readers may need to read such information more than once. Tell them:

- first, read each word separately to ensure it is decoded correctly – hide oncoming words with a finger to ensure that the eye does not move on too fast

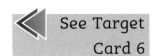
See Target
Card 6

- second, read to understand the sense.

Then ask the reader to put the information into his own words.

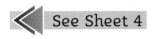
See Sheet 4

For more advanced readers who have essay, homework or exam questions, an additional stage is first **highlight** the **process**, and then <u>underline</u> the <u>content</u> words.

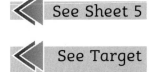
See Sheet 5

See Target
Card 7

Name the **three** largest cities in Europe. = **process**
Name the three <u>largest cities</u> in <u>Europe</u>. = <u>content</u>

Write down **four** of the **reasons** given for <u>conserving energy</u>.

Compare and **contrast** life for <u>workers</u> in <u>Victorian England</u> with the <u>present day</u>.

Describe the <u>main characters</u> in the <u>Merchant of Venice</u>.

This activity is particularly valuable when based on old test or exam papers.

4 Interactive reading

This type of reading, for which there are several methods, is described fully in Chapter 8.

Choosing which type of reading to do

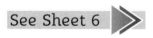

Once each type of reading has been mastered, students need practice in deciding when to use them.

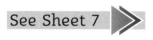

- Students can work in pairs to complete a quiz sheet together; this encourages discussion of why a method might be chosen.

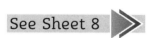

- Students can decide which of the four reading methods is appropriate for reading in class or for homework.

NB: Sometimes more than one method is appropriate.

Once completed, have a feedback session in which choices are justified.

Four questions will cover most purposes for reading. Ask these questions before reading.

Do I want:	Strategy needed
1 a general idea of the text?	Skimming text
2 a specific piece of information?	Scanning text for key words or symbols
3 to understand the exact meaning?	Accurate reading of every word
4 to learn and remember this?	Interactive reading (see Chapter 8) for in-depth knowledge and understanding and full recall

Time how long it it takes you to skim this article and find the key information.

The jeans success story

Levi Strauss is one of the world's largest brand name clothing companies. They manufacture and market jeans and casual sportswear using the following brand names; Levis, Dockers and Slates. The company has registered the Levis trademark in more than 200 countries.

Levis Strauss & Co. employ approximately 1600 staff at their San Francisco headquarter and another 30,000 people worldwide. They have 32 production facilities and 29 customer service centres throughout the world.

Levi history

Levi Strauss was a Bavarian immigrant who went to San Francisco in 1853. When he first arrived he was told he would need some hardwearing trousers, so he made some for himself out of canvas. This could be said to be the first pair of Levi jeans! Over the next twenty years he built up a very successful business selling dry goods and manufacturing work clothes which included 'waist overalls' that we know today as jeans.

When miners began to complain of torn pockets caused by the heavy gold nuggets they carried, Levi Strauss decided to develop a method of reinforcing the pockets. He enlisted the help of a tailor called Jacob W. Davis who came up with the idea of using a copper wire to rivet the pockets. The rivet was patented in 1873 and this was the start of rivets so familiar on today's jeans.

When Levis Strauss died in 1902 he left his thriving business to his four nephews. The family continue to control it today.

Levi's 501

Levi's 501 jeans were first created in the 1800s and were given the number 501 around 1890. They are distinguished by their button-fly and their Shrink-To-Fit nature. They are made from serge de Nimes denim, a type of cotton twill originally made in Nimes, France over 500 years ago. The denim is dyed blue with indigo (see opposite). In 1936 the Red Tab Device was created to help identify Levi's 501 jeans from a distance. These jeans were called waist overalls up until 1960.

Today Levi's 501 jeans are made in approximately 108 sizes with 20 different finishes and fabrics. The typical production for one pair requires 1¾ yards of denim and 213 yards of thread.

How many key facts did you remember?

From King, H. *Textiles Technology: the Clothing Industry*. Harcourt Education

Scanning

The Giant Panda is found in small areas of China. The male can grow to a height of 1.5 m and can weigh up to 120 kg. Pandas are very rare. They eat mainly bamboo, but also eat berries, fruit, flowers, fungi, grass, bark and sometimes birds' eggs. They need to eat many times each day (16 hours a day). They live in cold regions where bamboo grows.

Questions

1   Which country did the Giant Panda live in?

2   How many metres high might a Giant Panda be?

3   How many kilograms might a Giant Panda weigh?

4   How many hours of each day do Giant Pandas need to spend eating?

Read the following instructions accurately.

Remember:

● Read each word separately and slowly. Hold your finger or a ruler over the next words so that you only look at one at a time.

Inserting and Removing Diskettes

When using the floppy drive, always insert your floppy diskette with the label-side facing up. To remove the inserted diskette, press the eject button on the top-right corner of the floppy drive.

● Next read each sentence again and make sure you understand what it means.

● Now put the information into your own words.

From *User's Manual Notebook*, Section 2: 'Using the Computer'. 2–13

Examination questions

Show the key words which you will need in order to answer the questions accurately. **Highlight** the **process** words and <u>underline</u> the <u>content</u> words.

1   Name the four largest counties in the UK.

2   List the uses of copper.

3   Translate the passage into English.

4   Name the main characters in *Romeo and Juliet*.

5   Imagine you are Einstein at work and write a page from his diary.

6   Describe the painting, the *Mona Lisa*.

7   Write down all the things that you are good at.

8   Produce a brief explanation for the beginning of the Second World War.

9   List the properties of mercury.

10   Name three types of decoration the Viking women used on clothes.

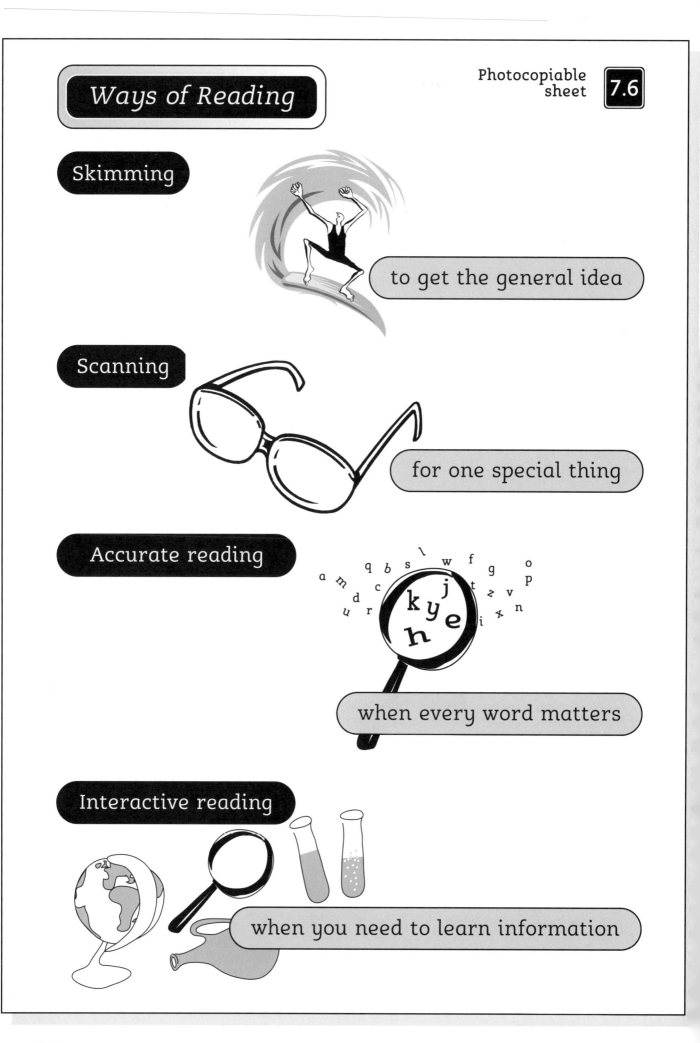

Ways of Reading

Skimming

to get the general idea

Scanning

for one special thing

Accurate reading

when every word matters

Interactive reading

when you need to learn information

Choosing a Reading Strategy

How would you read the following pieces of information?

Reading material – you need to know:	Skimming	Scanning	Accurate reading	Interactive reading
1 how a new DVD player works from the **manual**.				
2 when 'Friends' is on from the **television page** of the paper.				
3 what dates your exams are on from the overall **timetable**.				
4 if a **chapter** on birds is likely to help with your project.				
5 the part that the Nurse has in the plot of **'Romeo and Juliet'**.				
6 where to get a second-hand bike from the **'for sale' ads** in the local newspaper.				
7 the currency of Singapore in a **table of currencies**.				
8 the causes of the First World War for a history project.				
9 your doctor's phone number from a **telephone directory**. His name is Dr Ben Jones and his surgery is in Whitewell.				

Identify the reading method needed

Write down on the chart five pieces of reading that you have to do in school or for homework. Tick the type of reading that it involved. Remember there may be more than one method to choose.

Reading material	Skimming	Scanning	Accurate reading	Interactive reading
1				
2				
3				
4				
5				

How to skim text

Look at:

- title
- bold type
- any large print
- any pictures or illustrations
- diagrams and charts
- captions
- first and last sentence
- first and last paragraph.

What do you know now?

How to skim a whole book

Look at:

- title
- table of contents
- chapter headings
- introduction
- any brief summaries available
- any chapter which looks particularly promising.

Practising skimming

Take a newspaper article you have not read and skim read it in 30 seconds. Remember to look quickly at:

- title
- bold type
- any large print
- any pictures or illustrations
- any diagrams and charts
- any captions
- first and last sentence
- first and last paragraph.

Now say what you have learnt about the topic.

How to speed-read

- Read the whole of the first sentence.
- Then let the eyes run along each line of text, skimming the main words. (Sometimes moving the fingertip rapidly underneath the lines can help.)
- Finally, read the whole of the last sentence.

How much do you know now?

Target Reading Comprehension – 7 Types of Reading 123

Working on accurate reading

Find five different examples of text in your home, which would need **accurate reading**. You might look:

- in the kitchen (recipes? kitchen appliances? bus or train timetable?)
- in the bathroom (medicine packaging? face cream?)
- in the living room (board games? manual for TV or video recorder? letters?).

Working on accurate reading

Look at the instructions you have written for three different sorts of homework. Highlight the process words and underline the content words.

How to scan text

Before you start to scan, *think* what the information or word will look like.

- Is it likely to be long or short?
- Will it start with a capital letter?
- What is the first letter likely to be?
- Will there be a pattern in the letters?
- Will there be any numbers?

Now 'visualise' the information or word.
Scan with that in your 'mind's eye'.
Do not allow your eyes to focus on any distractions.
The rest of the text should seem quite vague and hazy.
If you are looking for a fact, think of the words it is likely to be near.

How to read instructions accurately

Read them twice.

- First time – read each word separately. Put a finger over the next words so you only look at the one you are reading.
- Second time – read to understand the sense.
- Now put the information into your own words.

Interactive Reading

8

Many readers read passively, i.e. it is an eye rather than a thinking exercise. Some may read accurately enough but fail to understand or recall what they have read.

These readers are often unaware that they are not extracting meaning from text. They lack **metacognitive awareness**.

> **Metacognitive awareness** is displayed when good readers keep track of comprehension and use conscious strategies to help them understand when they do not – for example backtracking, or checking out the meaning of a word.

Metacognitive awareness is encouraged through all the interactive reading methods presented in this chapter.

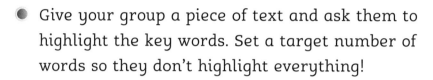

The following activities will highlight which readers are unable to read with full understanding.

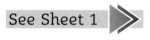 See Sheet 1

- Give your group a piece of text and ask them to highlight the key words. Set a target number of words so they don't highlight everything!

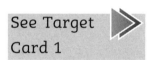 See Target Card 1

- Use Target Card 1 to give students practice in highlighting key words.

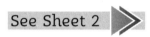 See Sheet 2

- Ask readers to **précis or summarise a piece of writing**; this can be subject-specific or general, e.g. a newspaper article. Give a target number of words to which the text should be reduced. A third to a half of the original number is sensible.

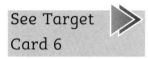 See Target Card 6

- Check that readers are monitoring comprehension by giving them a passage that contains wrong information and ask them to find any problems with the text.

See Sheet 3

RAP

A simple activity to alert students to the complex skill of reading with understanding is **RAP**. You can use the idea of rapping on a door to have it opened.

RAP is a three step action:

1 Read – first, you read the information, a piece at a time.

2 Ask yourself the question 'what is it all about?'.

3 Put it into your own words.

This RAP strategy is a straightforward way of inviting readers to interact with text. Each of the subsequent activities in this section is similar. Begin with RAP and then move on to more complex and detailed activities, depending on the age and stage of the reader.

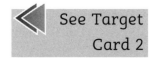
See Target Card 2

It is tempting to view RAP as basic, but it works with readers of all ages, particularly those who have never really understood that reading is more than turning words into sounds.

DARTs

DARTs* = Directed Activities Related to Texts.

DARTs activities promote independent reading beyond passive reading; they invite interaction with the text and this encourages understanding.

Choose activities to suit the kind of text being read:

1 Analysing text

a **Underlining or highlighting** – ask readers to underline or highlight everything in the text that refers to a particular theme or subject. For example, highlight all the words that describe a character in a piece of narrative, or all the arguments for a proposal in a debate.

b **Segmenting** – take a piece of continuous prose, take out the paragraph breaks and ask the readers to divide it into paragraphs.

c **Labelling** – label the segments from the activity above or label the paragraphs in another passage. Use a key word or phrase.

---

* See http://www.teachingenglish.org.uk/think/read/darts.shtml for more information and examples

d **Grouping and ranking** – group ideas together by colour coding or rank them in order of importance, e.g. put a famous person's achievements in order of importance, by numbering, 1, 2, 3, etc.

2 Recording and representing information from the text

This can be done after some of the activities in the previous section.

a **Listing** – having completed the underlining or highlighting exercise (on Sheet 1), ask the student to list the points. This is an important first step in note-taking, note-making and summarising.

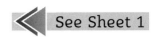 See Sheet 1

- *Either* ask students to read the passage on Sheet 4a and make headings and subheadings, *or* give them the headings and subheadings and ask them to fill in the details.

See Sheet 4a

- More capable students can tackle harder passages.

See Sheet 4b

b **Tables** – construct a table from information given in the text.

- First offer a skeleton table to be filled in; but after practice get the readers to construct their own tables.
- This is an excellent activity for group work.

The following table would suit a simple geographical text.

Name of town	Number of population	Main industries

Examples of science tables:

Mineral	Source	Function
Calcium	Cheese, milk	Bone formation

Vitamin	Name	Source	Function
A	Retinol	Fish oils, liver	Helps vision and night blindness

c **Diagrams** – flow diagrams / hierarchies/ networks / cartoons / pie charts / timelines.

- Turn prose into a diagram. This is an ideal way to get readers to focus on the meaning and structure of information.
- It also aids recall.
- Choosing the most suitable kind of diagram is an excellent thinking activity for more able students.

Flow diagrams work well for sets of procedures, instructions or sequences, e.g. how to make a cup of tea, or setting up the timer for a video programme.

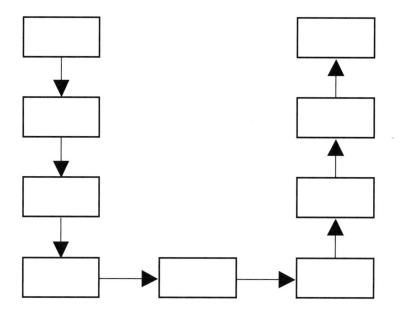

Water cycle:

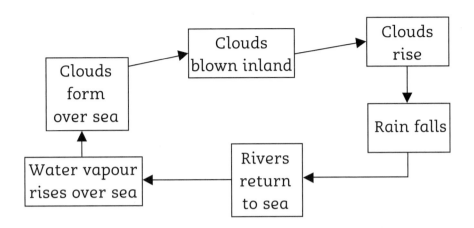

Pie charts can show proportions and percentages, e.g. aspects of weather throughout the year, water usage in the UK or sources of energy in African countries.

Cheese production percent by type, 1997

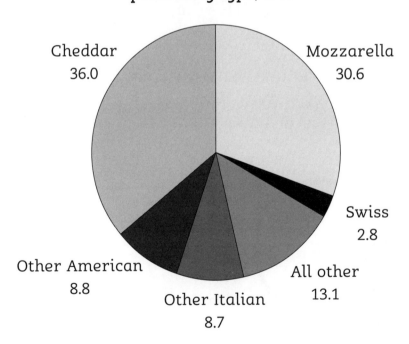

Hierarchies can be used for any information that has a hierarchical structure or a ranking order, e.g. the feudal system or family histories.

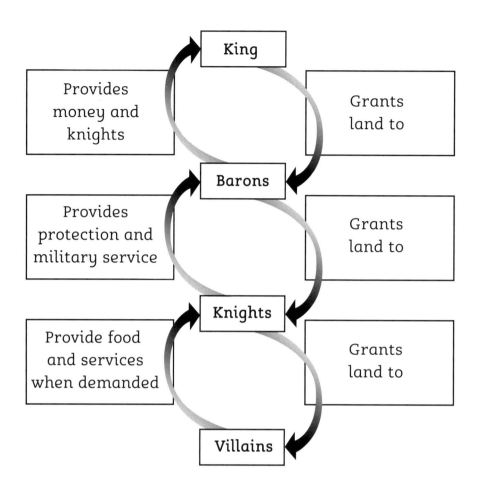

Timelines are excellent for overviews in History, particularly when it is useful to see what was happening in different parts of the world at the same time.

Venn diagrams are useful for looking at similarities and differences in characters, stories and poems, e.g. boys' and girls' pastimes.

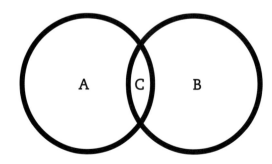

They are also suitable for 'compare and contrast' studies, e.g. 'What do these characters, or topics, have in common (C) and how they are distinctive (A and B).

Using boys' and girls' favourite pastimes:

A (pastimes that usually only boys have) might be football, skateboarding and Scalectrix

B (pastimes that usually only girls have) might be trying on make-up, looking at teen magazines, gymnastics

C (pastimes that both boys and girls have) might be cycling, pop music, swimming and watching videos.

More resources for work on diagrams

- Look at the Internet, good textbooks and publications by Dorling Kindersley for more ideas.

- Search for 'Graphic Organisers' on the Internet to find numerous applications for different representations of information.

- See also the *Oxford Headwork Series** for many examples of information presented in diagrams.

Having shown students examples of different ways of presenting information in diagram form, look at various texts and ask them to discuss which formats suit which kinds of information.

d **Questions** – provide questions to answer or ask students to formulate questions that the text answers.
- Refer to Chapter 6 for suggestions on question formulation to use before, during or after reading.

---

* Culshaw, Chris and Waters, Deborah, *Headwork*. OUP. ISBN 0-19-833372-2 (book 1), 0-19-833373-0 (book 2), 0-19-833374-9 (book 3) and 0-19-833375-7 (book 4)

● Use **Reciprocal Teaching*** resources to help pupils work independently and with each other to formulate useful questions.

3   Reconstruction of the text

a Completion

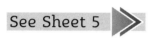

● Give text with particular kinds of words or phrases deleted. This is different from random cloze procedure where words are deleted in an arbitrary way.

● Delete meaningful words or phrases; these have to be filled in by the reader, requiring prior knowledge of the subject and reading skills.

b Sequencing sentences

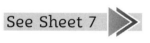

● Photocopy passages.

● Cut them into separate sentences for the readers to sequence logically.

● Compare them to the original.

● Discuss why the first sentence must be first (e.g. pronoun used later).

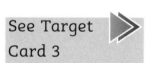

c Prediction – ask the group to predict what will come next. This can be done at any point, from the title through to any appropriate pausing point.

The passage in Sheet 7 comes early in *Friday Forever* by Annie Dalton**. It is an example of how readers could pause and discuss:

● the character

● what his parents might be like

● and what kind of a story might be expected to follow.

* Reciprocal teaching websites:

http://www.ncrel.org/sdrs/areas/issues/students/atrisk/at6lk38.htm

http://curry.edschool.virginia.edu/go/readquest/strat/rt.html

** Dalton, Annie, *Friday Forever*. Barrington Stoke

It is not important that the answers are correct as long as the reader is becoming involved with the characters and the plot.

More DARTs activities

See Sheets 8 and 9. Also use Sheets 12, 13 and 14 in Chapter 5 if you have not done so already.

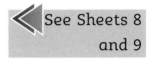

See Sheets 8 and 9

Mind mapping

Mind mapping* is another way of putting information into a different format. It is a great way of changing text into visual notes. It can be used to make notes from articles or chapters or even a whole book summary. It is a multi-sensory approach, aiding both comprehension and retention. Mind maps are easily turned back into continuous prose as the structure and sequence are retained. Each branch of the mind map becomes a paragraph with the key word on the branch being the key word in the topic sentence, stating the main point.

How to mind map

Preparation

- Begin with a piece of text which divides readily into sections. Read it and decide on a key word for each section.

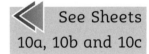

See Sheets 10a, 10b and 10c

- You need a large blank sheet of paper, highlighters and coloured pens.

- Highlight key words in each sentence. (Initially, state a maximum number of words to ensure these really are the key words.)

- Turn the paper sideways into the landscape position.

---

* Look at any of the numerous books by Tony Buzan on mind mapping, especially *Mind Maps for Kids: The Shortcut to Success at School*. HarperCollins (2003)

Getting started

- Draw a main central image as the 'title' – or write the title word large.

- Draw a branch from the main image for each section using separate colours.

- Write one key word in capitals on each branch – these are the titles of each section.

- From each main branch draw thinner branches in the same colour for the details.

- Add key words to sum up each detail – in clearly printed lower case.

Extending the mind map

- Use colour to make a point memorable.

- Draw pictures instead of using words whenever possible.

- Use signs and symbols too.

- Add importance by drawing a bubble around a word or making it bigger.

- Get creative!

Advantages of mind maps

- Use the whole brain.

- The act of drawing the lines unblocks the mind and opens up pathways.

- Simple and enjoyable.

- Highly individual to suit personal style.

- Whole subject on one page.

- The brain is active when creating a mind map – information is processed and understood.

- Can be used for review and revision.

SKWL

SKWL, an adaptation of **KWL***, is another good strategy to help comprehension.

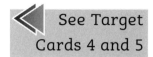

See Target Cards 4 and 5

Model it as a classroom activity several times before students are expected to do it on their own. Present a text and take your students through the following stages:

- **Skim** – here it is useful to refer to the TCP strategy devised by Neil Mackay.**

TCP stands for:

T – Title

- What is this all about?
- How does it fit in?

C – Captions

- Anything that is in bold?
- Anything that catches the eye?
- Context clues?
- What is it about?

P – Picture

- Look at any photographs or illustrations.

- **Know** – what do you know about this topic already? This activates prior knowledge.

- **Want** – what do you want to know or what will the teacher want you to know? This activates questions to help focus reading. Now you are ready to read.

- **Learn** – what have you learned? Discuss this after the piece has been read.

---

* Ogle, D.M. (1986) 'K-W-L: A teaching model that develops active reading of expository text'. *Reading Teacher*, 39, 564–570

** Neil Mackay, Action Dyslexia Training and Consultancy (info@actiondyslexia.co.uk)

See Sheet 11a

Students may prefer blank grids for KWL – see Sheet 11a.

KWL activity

See Sheets 11a and 11b

- Ask students what they **know** about Mexico City. They can write this on Sheet 11a or record group responses on the board or flip chart.

- Ask students what they **want** to know. Record responses.

- Ask students to read Sheet 11b.

- Supply any words that they do not know.

- Tell them to use Sheet 11a to record what they have learned.

- At the end summarise with the group what they have **learned**.

See Sheet 12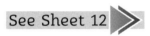

SQ3R

- Many students now use this technique to read more efficiently.

- It is how some of us read unconsciously but needs to be taught to many students.

- It is useful for longer texts.

- It builds on earlier strategies and will suit only the more able students.

- It can also incorporate strategies such as mind mapping at the recall stage.

- Guide students through the following with appropriate passages.

Survey

Tell students to survey the material quickly to get a general idea of the whole and to identify relevant sections. Skim:

- the contents page and index
- introductions
- headings
- diagrams
- conclusions.

Question

- Encourage them to ask some definite questions in order to give purpose to their reading.

- Assist at this stage by supplying helpful questions.

Read

- Tell students to read in detail, possibly a section at a time.

- Ask them to look for the main ideas of a chapter or section. These are often found in the first or final paragraph.

- Tell them to read 2 or 3 times rapidly **or** once slowly, whatever is best for them individually – let them experiment.

Recall

- Tell students to consider carefully what they have just read and decide what the main points were.

- Ask them to take notes in their own words of main ideas and important facts if they want to.
  NB: They should not make notes until they have read the whole section and can decide what the main points are.

Review

- Ask students to look back over what they have read and check their notes.

- This is when they should evaluate what they have read.

Highlight or underline approximately 40 of the most important words in the following paragraph.

Hint: there are 79 words in this paragraph. That means you highlight or underline about half of them.

Population rise

In many countries the death rate is now lower than the birth rate. That means there are more babies born than people dying. This will make the population rise. In many poor countries it is rising very quickly. This will lead to many extra people in these countries. They will need places to live and food to eat. They need health care and education. If the population grows too quickly, some poor countries will find it difficult to cope.

Writing a Summary

Read the following passage and summarise it in about 85–95 words. There are 193 words in the passage.

The *Titanic*: a new British ship began its first trip across the Atlantic Ocean on April 10th, 1912. It left England to sail to New York. The *Titanic* was the largest and most beautiful ship in the world at that time.

The ship was said to be so safe that it could not sink. Yet on the fifth night at sea, it hit an iceberg and sank in less than three hours. The iceberg was seen just before the crash, but the ship was going too fast to steer away from it. When the ship struck the iceberg, it made a big hole where seawater came in quickly.

The *Titanic* did not have enough lifeboats for its 2,200 passengers. In fact, the lifeboats had room for less than half of them. The crew tried to send women and children into the lifeboats first. More than 1,500 people drowned when the *Titanic* sank.

Because of poor radio contact the *Titanic* could not get enough help from other ships in time. The *Carpathia*, another British ship, did get the call for help. It sped through the ice and saved all the people it could find.*

* Einstein, C. (2001) *Reading for Content, Book 1*. Educators Publishing Service. ISBN 0-8388-1651-7.

Wrong Information

Read the following paragraph and underline all the wrong information that you find.

The Thomsons had just arrived at the seaside. They opened their sunroof in the car and left it in the car park. It was a hot and sunny day, so they put on their gloves and made sure they had their umbrellas with them. They decided to have lunch, as it was ten o'clock in the morning. As Mrs Thomson was a vegetarian they chose to go to the hamburger bar. Mr Thomson and the children ordered fish and chips and Mrs Thomson chose a bacon butty. The bill was for 25 pence and Mr Thomson complained about how expensive eating out had become in the 21st century. They went to the beach which was lovely and grassy. They paddled in the water and when they discovered how icy cold it was they thought it would be perfect for a swim. They put on all their clothes and swam happily for the next ten hours. Because they were not tired they stopped and went home. They all agreed that they had had a miserable day.

Living in Greece

Many Greeks are farmers. They grow crops like wheat, tobacco, cotton, apples and grapes on the plains where the soil is good. Farmers also keep sheep and goats for their milk which is made into cheese.

Most Greeks wear clothes like yours. Some older Greeks wear black when they go out. Women wear black shawls. They wear black to show respect for members of the family who have died.

Most Greeks live in the country. Their homes usually have four or five rooms, flat roofs and white-washed walls. Greek houses often have verandas. Vines along the tops of the verandas give shade from the sun.*

Fill in the details.

1 Farming in Greece

    a   Crops grown

    b   Animals reared

2 Clothes in Greece

    a   What most Greeks wear

    b   What older Greeks wear

3 Houses in Greece

    a   Where most people live

    b   Country houses

---

* *A Visit to Greece*, Peter and Connie Roop. Heinemann, ISBN 0-431-08288-X.

Headings and Subheadings

Read the passage. Fill in the details under the headings and subheadings given at the end of the passage.

Different kinds of musical instruments

There are many kinds of musical instruments. We can divide them into three types, depending on the way they are played.

Some musical instruments are played by striking or banging them. These instruments are called percussion instruments One example is the drum. There are many different kinds of drums.

Some musical instruments are played by blowing air into them. They are called wind instruments. Sometimes the air vibrates inside a wooden tube. These instruments belong to the woodwind group. The clarinet, the flute and the bassoon are examples of woodwind instruments. Some other wind instruments are made of brass, for example the trumpet and the horn. There are other kinds of wind instruments like the bagpipes and the mouth organ.

The third type of musical instruments are those with strings. There are two kinds of stringed instruments. The first one is where the player draws a bow across the strings for example the violin and the cello. The second kind of stringed instrument are those where plucking the strings makes the music. Examples of these are the harp and the guitar.

Headings and subheadings

1 Percussion instruments
    a) Drum
2 Wind instruments
    a) Woodwind e.g.
    b) Brass
    c) Others
3 Stringed instruments
    a) Played with a bow
    b) Played by plucking

Cloze

Read the following paragraph and fill in the gaps with words that would make sense in the context.

I switched off the video and dressed for school. Tuesday is "can't wait" day. It's straight downstairs, sneak past Mum's and Amber's

_____ , and don't make a _____ on the creaking

floorboard to _____ the dog. Pull the magazine out of the letter

_____ and stuff your fingers in the letter box flap to stop it

shutting with a _____ . Then fly upstairs as fast and as quietly

as you can clutching the _____ tight in your fist. Close your

_____ door without a _____ and then breathe more

easily. Open the fingers of your _____ for your fist full of

football fantasy and magic. For _____ is the day of SCORE and

its free football sticker.*

* Goodwin, John, *Nice One, Sam*. Oxford University Press.

Sequencing

(To be cut up by the teacher.)

Arrange the cut up sentences you have been given into the correct order.

The college has formed a new orchestra and put on a concert last week.

Dave chose to play the kettledrums.

Kettledrums are called Timpani.

He likes to play them as they make such loud noise.

He does not always remember to look at the conductor.

At the concert last week he missed a beat early in the first piece of music.

The performance of the piece ended with a loud Timpani solo.

The composer had not written this.

Prediction

Read the passage and answer your teacher's questions.

Ever seen anyone blow up a balloon, then let it go? The balloon goes crazy. It goes right out of control. It zooms around the room screaming.

Well, that's how I felt inside. I felt as if there was a balloon inside me, filled with way too much air.

If I wasn't careful, if I didn't hold it in really, really tight, it might go zooming out of control. I might do something crazy, even dangerous.

I told you I was under pressure. Major Pressure. And where was all this pressure coming from? My parents, who else?*

---

* Dalton, Annie, *Friday Forever*. Barrington Stoke

Key Words and Making a Table

Read the following passages and then do the activities underneath.

What is a dinosaur?

The name 'dinosaur' means 'terrible lizard'. Dinosaurs were given their names because they look a bit like the lizards alive today. But dinosaurs died out 65 million years ago, and they were different from lizards and other living reptiles. They could walk on straight legs tucked under their bodies, instead of out at the side. This meant they could walk further, move faster and grow bigger than any other reptiles.

- Underline or highlight 20 key words.

Reptiles and amphibians

The best way to tell the difference between a reptile and an amphibian is to look at their skin. Reptiles, such as snakes and crocodiles have dry, scaly skin. Amphibians such as frogs and salamanders, have wet smooth skin. Both reptiles and amphibians have a bony skeleton, and their bodies are the same temperature as their surroundings. Most of them live in warm places.*

- Underline or highlight 20 key words.

- Write a sentence to say what this is telling you about reptiles and amphibians.

- Use the following table to show how dinosaurs are similar to and different from lizards.

Similarities	Differences

* Taylor, B. (2001) *Oxford First Book of Dinosaurs*. Oxford University Press.

Read the following information and fill in the table below.

What can we recycle?

Bottle banks are found in many local council areas and are divided into those accepting clear, green and brown glass. Blue glass can be put into the green bank and clear glass with coloured coatings can be put into the clear bank, as the coating will burn off. The labels on bottles and jars will be removed during the recycling process, however remove as many plastic or metal rings and tops as possible. Only recycle bottles and jars, never light bulbs, sheet glass or Pyrex-type dishes as these are made from a different type of glass.*

- Fill in the table below to show what you **can** put into each bottle bank.

- In the last column list the items that you must **not** put into any bottle bank.

Clear	Green	Brown	Not allowed

* Waste Watch, www.wastewatch.org.uk

How to Mind Map

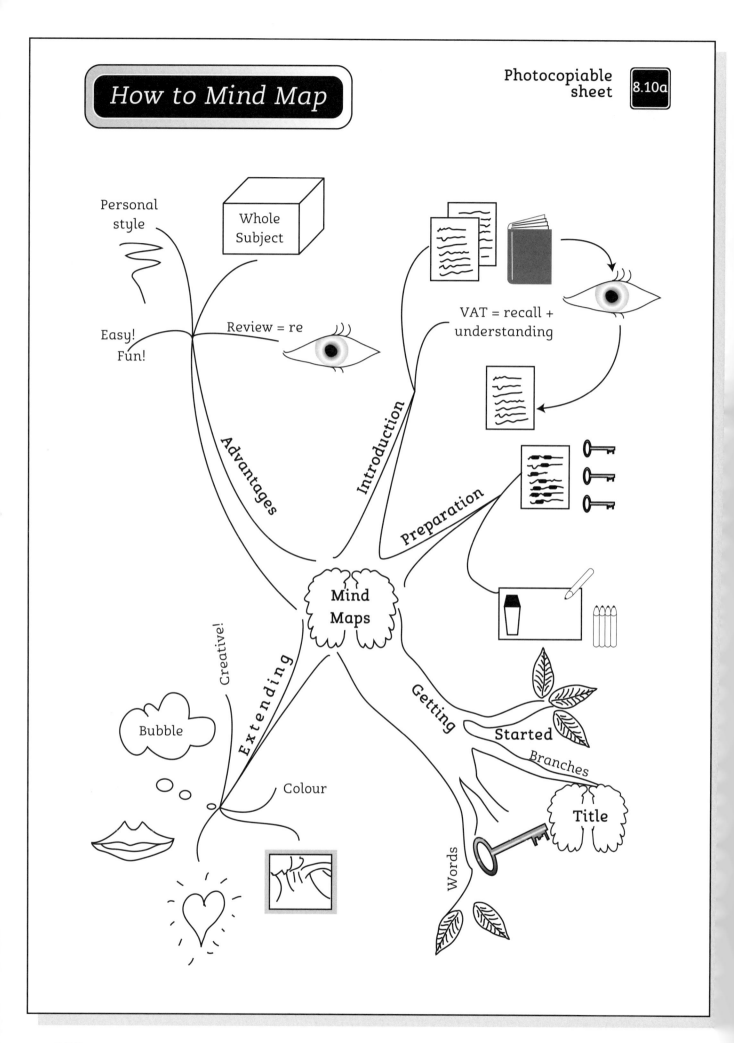

Make a Mind Map

Turn the following information into a mind map.

In 1665 the Lord Mayor gave these orders to all Londoners to try to stop the plague from spreading:

- Examiners: To enquire what houses be visited [by illness] and what persons be sick, and of what diseases. And if they find any person sick of the infection the house shall be shut up for a month and none can leave the house. Every house infected to be marked with a red cross a foot long with these words: 'Lord Have Mercy Upon Us'.

- Searchers: Women searchers to be appointed. They shall make a search and report whether the persons do die of the infection, or of what other diseases. No searcher be permitted to keep any shop or stall, or work as a laundress.

- Watchmen: For every infected house there be appointed watchmen, one for the day, and the other for the night. They have a special care that no person goes in or out of infected houses.

- Householders: Every householder must keep the street before his door swept all the week long.

- Rakers and dog-killers: The filth of houses be daily carried away by the rakers. No dogs, cats or conies [rabbits] to be kept in the city. Dogs to be killed by the dog-killers.

- The burial of the dead must be always before sunrise or after sunset. No friend can accompany the corpse to church upon pain of having his house shut up. All the graves shall be at least six feet deep.*

---

* Shephard, Hinton, Hite and Lomas (1992) *Societies in Change*. John Murray.

Mind Map

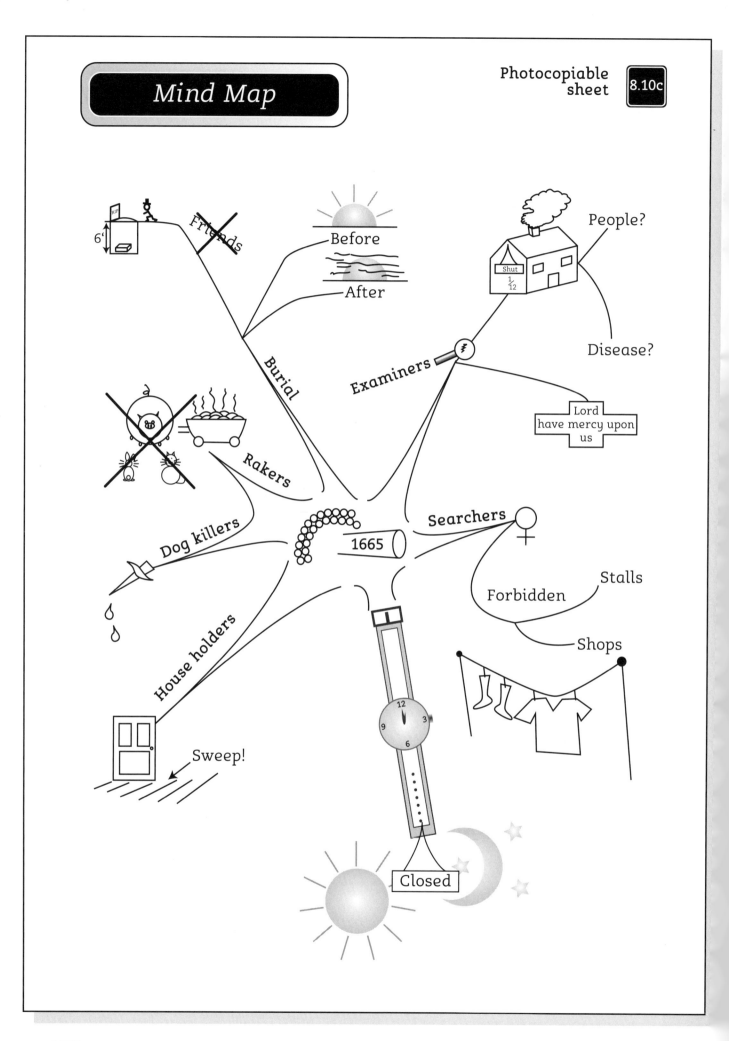

Friends

Before

After

People?

Shut 1/12

Disease?

Burial

Examiners

Lord have mercy upon us

6' RIP

Rakers

Dog killers

1665

Searchers

House holders

Forbidden

Stalls

Shops

Sweep!

Closed

Grid for KWL

K	W	L
What do you know?	What do you want to know?	What have you learned?

Mexico City

Problems in the largest city in the world

What do you know about the largest city in the world?

Mexico City has many problems. By the year 2000 its population is expected to reach more than 25 million, and it is likely to be the largest city in the world. Thousands of people arrive each day from poor country areas. The newcomers have to live in appalling slums on the edge of the city. Because there is little work, children are sent into the streets to earn what they can.

The streets are crammed with cars and these together with hundreds of factories, have created an immense pollution problem. The city is often covered by a dark grey mist. There is also a shortage of water, as Mexico City is not built near a river. Finally the lake bed, on which the city is built has become unstable, partly as a result of earthquakes and tremors. Some of the city's buildings are gradually sinking.*

* Marison, Marion, *Discovering Mexico*. A Zoe Book. ISBN 1-874488-60-6

SQ3R

Survey

Survey the material quickly to get a general idea of the whole and to identify relevant sections.

Skim

- the contents page and index
- introductions
- headings
- diagrams
- conclusions
- bibliography.

Question

Ask yourself some questions in order to give a more definite purpose to your reading.

Read

- detailed reading, possibly a section at a time
- look for the main ideas of a chapter or section which are often in the first or final paragraph
- read two or three times rapidly **or** once slowly – whichever is the best for you – experiment.

Recall

Consider carefully what you have just read - what were the main points? Take notes in your own words of main ideas and important facts but do not start making notes until you have read the whole section.

Review

A quick look back over what you have read and check your notes.

This is the point at which you should be able to evaluate what you have read.

Highlight key words

- Work with a partner.
- Take a piece of writing from any of your texts about 200 words in length.
- Highlight approximately 50–60 key words.
- Compare your highlighted words with the words that your partner has highlighted.

RAP is a 3 step action

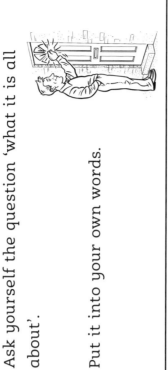

1. Read – first, you read the information, a piece at a time.
2. Ask yourself the question 'what it is all about'.
3. Put it into your own words.

Traffic lights

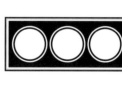

When you are reading, pause every now and again.

Stop

Think: What has happened so far?
What might happen next?
What do I think about the story and the characters?

Start reading and see if you were right.

Use this traffic lights technique every time you are reading. It keeps you alert.

KWL

Do K and W before I read.

K What do I know?

W What do I want to know?

Do L after I read.

L What have I learned?

SKWL

S Skim the page for a few moments.
Remember: **TCP – Title, Captions, Pictures**.

What have you found out?

K What do you **know** already about the topic?

W What do you **want** to know about the topic?

Now read the passage carefully.

L What have you **learned**?

Summarise this passage

Your target number of words is

_____

Time how long it takes you.

_____ minutes

Visualisation

Visualisation is making pictures 'in the head' or 'in the mind's eye'. These pictures may be still, like a photograph, or moving, like a video. They may be in black and white or colour. Visualisation can take place while listening or thinking or reading. It is valuable when reading as it helps with:

- understanding
- sequence
- time order
- memory
- recall.

A picture is worth a thousand words

Some readers, especially dyslexic readers, may have better visual than verbal abilities. This may be shown by: artistic talent; the ability to draw well or to remember what they have seen; a preference for teaching in which there is plenty of visual stimulation etc. These readers may find visualisation particularly helpful. All readers do well to use visualisation as support for memory.

ASSESSMENT

Ask students to make pictures in their heads of:

- a film they have seen recently
- their favourite outfit
- a well-known pop star or footballer
- their bedroom at home
- what they had for breakfast
- their trip to school that morning.

Then ask them to describe their pictures. This is visual recall of what they have actually seen.

If a student has difficulty, make the task narrower by asking for a description of something more immediate:

- their school uniform
- the room in which they are sitting
- their school bag
- their best friend.

You may need to ask them to look first, then close their eyes and give a description from their visual memory.

Ask them to think about size, shape, colour, background, proportions and any special details.

Finally, ask students to read some descriptive prose or poetry, pausing after each sentence or every few lines, to think of the picture the words create in their 'mind's eye'. Ask them about the pictures they see. This is visualisation using imagination.

If students find visualisation difficult, use a more formal assessment of visual skills. Peeramid 2 (Pediatric Examination of Educational Readiness at Middle Childhood) is for the age range 9–15 years. The test includes a section on Visual Processing Functions. PEEX 2 (Pediatric Early Elementary Examination) is a similar battery of tests for ages 6–9 years.

Both tests are published by Educators Publishing Service, www.epsbooks.com, and are obtainable from the Helen Arkell Dyslexia Centre, Frensham, Farnham, Surrey GU10 3BW Tel: 01252 797511.

ACTIVITIES

Encourage students to think of visualisation as having a camera in their heads. Tell them the brain is amazing and can make all kinds of pictures. We can have pictures of real objects or events that have happened to us. We can imagine the future or even things which cannot possibly be real. If we apply this to reading, it can help us to understand and remember.

Tell them it may also help them to remember if they turn the pictures in their heads into simple drawings which can then become permanent notes.

Instructions

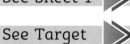

- Give each student a list of actions to read.

- Give them instructions on how to remember them using visualisation.

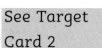

- Ask students to describe and draw aliens.

Barrier exercises

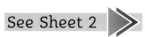

- Give students matching sets of coloured pens or pencils and a ruler.

- Place a barrier between them so they cannot see each other's paper.

- Ask students in turn to write a simple instruction,

e.g. Draw a small green square in the top left-hand corner. (The size can be specified, such as 2 cm wide.)

- The instruction is then passed to his partner.
- Students read and visualise the instruction, and place it face down.
- Both students draw what is required.
- After four instructions each, stop!
- Remove the barrier and compare pictures.
- They should be the same.

Reading and making pictures

- Take text which has plenty of description and visual 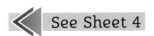 vocabulary. Ask students to read slowly and pause frequently to visualise.
- Look in textbooks or current literature to find suitable texts. Once students can visualise when reading passages with plenty of visual words they will be able to move on to general text.

Converting text to simple pictures

Converting text to mind maps is covered in Chapter 8 – 'Interactive Reading'.

Another way of linking visualisation to reading is to draw See Sheet 4 simple pictures suggested by the text. These might be doodles in the margin of a book owned by the student. Encourage this! It is often the doodles which are easier to recall and they remind the student of the content.

For instance, the gist of the following passage might be recalled by the accompanying line drawings.

Home receptions

If you (or willing members of your family) have a large enough home with outside space for a marquee, then your luck is very much in. It is incredible how many gardens, and indeed houses, there are around in which a marquee can be built. The benefits of a home wedding are that you can make it your own from the start to finish, it can be as high or low key as you want, and it can sometimes offer you the opportunity to save money.

The downside is that you really do have to start from scratch. You will have to hire catering equipment, caterers and furniture, and arrange car parking, toilets and a power supply, not to mention a whole host of other practicalities.

Taken from *Wedding Day Bridal Bible* edited by Kathryn Seidl (Beach Magazines and Publishing)

Sequencing information to make sense

See Sheet 5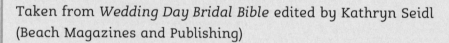

See Target
Card 3

Give students some sentences describing an event or an activity. Each should be written on a different slip of paper. Tell them to shuffle the slips, then to read and visualise each one. Finally they can put the slips in the correct order and read the story to a partner.

Activities which are suitable:

- getting ready for an exam
- texting a friend
- going to a concert
- taking a book out of the library
- planning a trip to the cinema with friends
- getting supper ready.

Actions

Set 1

Turn around in your chair to face behind you.

Wave your arm high in the air.

Point straight ahead with your arm outstretched.

Now tap both knees gently.

Raise both feet from the ground and put them down again.

Turn back to face the front.

Set 2

Point to your left ear.

Clasp both your hands together.

Touch your elbows with your hands.

Look to the left and then to the right.

Shut your eyes and open them again.

Barrier Exercise

- Work with a partner.

- Make sure you have matching sets of coloured pens or pencils and a ruler.

- Place a barrier between you so you cannot see each other's paper. (A large book or file might do.)

- One of you write a simple instruction, e.g. draw a small green square, 2 centimetres wide, in the top left-hand corner.

- Pass this to your partner.

- Both of you visualise the instruction, and place it face down.

- Both of you draw what it said.

- Repeat with the other person writing the next instruction.

- After 4 instructions each, stop!

- Remove the barrier and compare pictures.

- They should be the same.

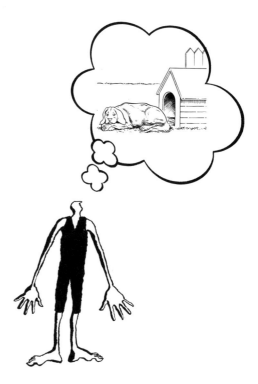

Read the following passage pausing frequently to make pictures in your head, imagining the scene. Your pictures can be still like a photograph or moving like a video. Make them as clear and as detailed as you can.

~ ✳ ❤ ✳ ~

He was riding on the back of an eagle owl, soaring through the clear blue sky towards an old, ivy-covered house set high on a hillside. Lower and lower they flew, the wind blowing pleasantly in Harry's face, until they reached a dark and broken window in the upper storey of the house, and entered. Now they were flying along a gloomy passageway, to a room at the very end ... through the door they went, into a dark room where the windows were boarded-up ...

Harry had left the owl's back ... he was watching, now, as it fluttered across the room, into a chair with its back to him. There were two dark shapes on the floor beside the chair ... both of them were stirring ... .

One was a huge snake ... the other was a man ... a short balding man, a man with watery eyes and a pointed nose ... he was wheezing and sobbing on the hearth-rug ... .

~ ✳ ❤ ✳ ~

When you have finished reading and imagining the pictures, turn over the page and recall the scene. Tell someone as much as you can remember.

"Harry Potter & the Goblet of Fire" Copyright © J.K. Rowling 2000

Read this passage slowly and visualise as you read. When you have finished, make some simple line drawings to remind you of the text. Tomorrow look at the line drawings only and see how much you can recall of what the text was about.

~ ✳ ❤ ✳ ~

There are two-headed creatures and three-headed creatures that have been found living in caves, high up in the Rocky Mountains. They are known for their acute hearing but both only have two large pink ears. The two-headed creatures or Bisects are vegetarians and mainly eat grass. The three-headed creatures or Trisects are meat eaters and live mainly on rabbits. On average Bisects live ten years longer than Trisects, which usually die when they are twenty years old. A team of international scientists is planning to carry out a study of these previously undiscovered creatures. They plan to catch two of each type, a male and a female. The males have long bushy tails and the females have short fluffy ones.

~ ✳ ❤ ✳ ~

See Target Card 3 for instructions to student

Give the student the following sentences on slips of paper in random order.

Going for a swim.

She stood deciding for a moment or two whether she really wanted this swim.

After a while she scrambled out of the pool shivering with cold.

Megan packed her swimmers into her sports bag and set off for the outdoor pool.

Megan changed, dived in and swam half a dozen lengths.

When she got there a notice on the door said 'Sorry, the heating system has failed! Half price entry today only'.

When she had dressed, she had a steaming hot cup of chocolate to drink.

Well, yes, she did want a swim and it was quite a sunny day.

Drawing an alien

Write a description of an alien in short sentences.

Example:

My alien is short and round.

He has two heads.

His body has yellow and red horizontal stripes.

In each head there are three eyes.

On top of his heads there are several antennae.

Now:

● swap descriptions with a partner

● read your partner's description

● after each sentence, pause and make a picture in
your head

● at the end, turn over the page

● draw the alien.

How to remember the actions

● Read the actions on sheet 9.1.

● Pause after each one and imagine/visualise
yourself carrying out the task.

● Make your images as clear as you can – take
your time.

● Now turn over the paper.

● Carry out the whole set of actions in order.

● Look back at the written actions to check if you
remembered them correctly.

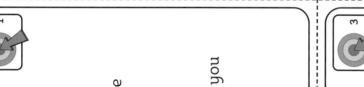

Reordering information to make sense

● Shuffle the strips of paper.

● Read each slip and visualise it.

● Put the slips into order to make a logical story.

● Read the story to your partner.

Reader's Toolkit

This final chapter gives suggestions for the teacher to discuss with a student. Students who understand their problems are more empowered to overcome them.

Read these bullet points with your student.

- Reading is probably one of the most difficult things we have to learn to do when we come to school.

- Some students seem to learn this skill easily. For others, it seems a great struggle.

- Sometimes, when readers are struggling, their teachers give them more books, usually easier books and tell them to practise reading. If reading is hard, this may seem like a punishment rather than a help.

- Readers can learn to read more effectively if they have help to discuss where the real problem is and how to work it out. They can then work on small problem areas rather than the big skill of reading.

- There is a checklist is to help build up a reading toolkit just for you. This will help you to get better and better at reading.

There are some questions on the checklist on the following pages for your student to think about and explanations for you to give them. Read it with your student and work out targets for reading practice together.

Checklist for reader to use with teacher support

Points for the reader to consider	Things to think about, things to do and targets to set for the reader	Possible Action Points for teacher and suggestions for the readers
• Can I see the print clearly or is it blurred? • Do I lose my place in the line of print or when moving to the next line? • Do I have to use my finger to point at each word? • Do I hold my book close to my eyes or have to screw my eyes up when reading?	If the answer is yes to **any** of these questions in this section, it might mean you need an eye check. If you cannot see very well, then you will find reading difficult. Don't worry, it does not mean you are going blind! Looking at words in books is a very different kind of eye activity to most of the looking we do in life. Talk to your teacher and get advice about the kind of vision specialist who would be best to check your eyes.	*There is more information about this kind of problem in Chapter 5 – TRA. Help your student to choose some Target Cards to work on from this chapter.*
• Does my teacher say I leave little words out when I am reading or confuse small words?	If I leave little words out or confuse them, tracking exercises might help.	*See exercises in Chapter 4 – TRA, Sheets 4.3, 4.9 and 4.10.*
• I find it difficult to remember new words. The rest of the class see new words and remember them quickly. I think there is something wrong with my memory.	We all have different kinds of memory, e.g. you remember people's faces, what your house looks like, what time your favourite programme is on, etc. Memory for words and the order of letters in words is another kind of memory. For some it works easily. For others it takes a bit more practice, just like learning to ride a bike! Look out for written words at all times. They are not just in books. They are all around you, on posters, shop windows, notices on walls etc. Aim to become a good noticer of words and even if	*Introduce your student to activities in Chapter 4 – TRA.* *Together, you can decide on targets that he can work on, to help build this kind of memory. Work on easy, common words before you move on to difficult words that he does not see very often.* *Add Sheet 7.2, Chapter 7 – TRA to his personal reader's toolkit to remind him of good ways to remember new words.*

Cont'd

Checklist for reader to use with teacher support

Points for the reader to consider	Things to think about, things to do and targets to set for the reader	Possible Action Points for teacher and suggestions for the readers
	you don't know what they are, you can sometimes guess what they say. Sometimes there are picture or symbol clues to help you guess. That's how you work out which toilet to use!	
• I find sounding out words very difficult. • I find long words difficult.	This could be because you find dealing with sounds difficult. Your brain deals with many sounds that your ears hear. Listening to music or cars go by is a very different activity from listening to sounds in words. Whole words can be much easier, especially if you understand what they mean. If you listen to *elephant*, you probably think of the animal rather than the combination of sounds *el-e-phant*. Teachers like you to sound words out because that helps you to work out words that you have never seen before. As you may have noticed, some words are easier to sound out than others.	It is best to check out your reader's skill with listening to sounds before you move on to looking at what the sounds look like when they are turned into letters. *Chapter 3 – TRA (Phonological Awareness and Phonics) is the best place to begin work on improving sounding out. Then you can add Sheet 1, Chapter 7 in TRA to his personal reader's toolkit to remind him of 'What to do if you don't know a word'.*
• I really don't enjoy reading. • The last thing I want to do is pick up a book. • The library is the last place I want to go to.	This is a shame because you have have not yet discovered that books can be great and a really good way of passing the time. Maybe this is because you have not yet found a good book that will really absorb you and take you off to a different world, a bit like going to a really good film.	

Cont'd

Checklist for reader to use with teacher support

Points for the reader to consider	Things to think about, things to do and targets to set for the reader	Possible Action Points for teacher and suggestions for the readers
• I really don't enjoy reading. • The last thing I want to do is pick up a book. • The library is the last place I want to go to.	Some people think reading is better than going to a film because you can make better pictures in your head. Good readers make good pictures in their heads. That is why you sometimes hear that people are disappointed when they go to a film of a book that they have read e.g. *Harry Potter* or *Lord of the Rings*, because the pictures in their heads were different ones! Never mind, there is plenty that we can suggest to help you like reading much more. Look at **non-fiction books** with good illustrations.	**Non-fiction books** – There are fewer words to read and there is a lot of information in the pictures and diagrams. Look at books about topics of high interest. Then your reader will have information in his mind already which will help him work out difficult bits. Another good thing about non-fiction is he can just read bits, and not have to start at the beginning and go right through to the end. The **Internet** is excellent for those who have had such a bad experience of books that they cannot bear to pick one up. Some kinds of software such as
	Look at the **Internet**. Search for things you want to know about and you will find an enormous amount of information about anything you can think of. Many adults who have to read a lot for their work find this an easy way to get information.	

Cont'd

Checklist for reader to use with teacher support

Points for the reader to consider	Things to think about, things to do and targets to set for the reader	Possible Action Points for teacher and suggestions for the readers
• I really don't enjoy reading. • The last thing I want to do is pick up a book. • The library is the last place I want to go to.	Maybe books are too hard or if they are easy they are too boring. If this is the case you might be able to work out whether you are reading the right level of book.	Text Help from IANSYST can read information to them. Finding the **right level** of reading is crucially important. *Look at Chapter 6 in TRA.* Books may be too hard or, if easy enough, they may be too babyish. Look out for publishers who sell books of high interest but low reading age. Discuss with your reader that writers can say things in a complicated way or more simply. Many of us prefer the simple version, e.g. *car* instead of *automobile.*
	You can find the right level with the five-finger exercise. Find a text of about 100 words and hold up one finger for each word you cannot read. If you hold up five fingers the text is too hard. Other things to try are: **visualisation**, that is, making pictures in your head as you read, and **listening to stories on tape** which will help you increase your vocabulary. Books have many more words in them than you will hear talking to your friends or watching soap operas on TV.	*Teach the five-finger exercise from Chapter 6 in TRA and add the corresponding target card to his toolkit, if that is appropriate.* Look at ways of reading from Chapter 6 in TRC. Chapter 9 in TRC gives practice in visualisation. Use Sheets 9.1, 9.2 and 9.3 for building this skill. Guide the student to interesting stories on tape/CD. Find videos of texts he is studying.

Cont'd

Checklist for reader to use with teacher support

Points for the reader to consider	Things to think about, things to do and targets to set for the reader	Possible Action Points for teacher and suggestions for the readers
	Once you find the right kind of reading it becomes a pleasant activity and a whole new world is open to you. Notice people on trains, buses and planes with their noses stuck into books. There must be a good reason for this!	
• I can read OK but I don't really understand it very well.	Good, you have made an excellent start to reading. You can turn the print on the page into the words that they say. Now onto the next stage, which is building up understanding. You need to think about where exactly understanding is difficult to find out where you need to begin.	Guide your student through the following comments in the next section 'Why understanding is difficult'.
Why understanding is difficult		
• I do not understand many of the words.	Sometimes writers use difficult words, e.g. *congenial* instead of *good fun*, *vocabulary* instead of *words*. Make sure the level of book is right for you. You may need to build up your vocabulary. Also, you can learn good ways of guessing what a word means from other clues in the sentence or the page. Good readers often guess and use clues to work out new words.	Check that he has the right level of text. *See Chapter 6 in TRA.* For vocabulary extension begin with activities in Chapter 3 – TRC. Guessing from context is an activity in Chapter 4 – TRC. See Sheet 4.1 – 'Words in Context' and you might suggest Target Card 1.

Checklist for reader to use with teacher support

Points for the reader to consider	Things to think about, things to do and targets to set for the reader	Possible Action Points for teacher and suggestions for the readers
• I understand the words as I go along but by the time I get to the end of the sentence I am not sure what it all means.	Sometimes sentences are too long or the words are in a difficult order. Working through different kinds of sentences will make you familiar with how to sort out what the writer means.	There is useful help for this in Chapter 4 in TRC. Look at Target Cards 2, 3 and 4 . Maybe, start with one and build up, when ready.
• I can answer the questions when the information is on the page, but sometimes the questions ask me what I think about something. I don't do as well with those questions.	That's well worked out and means that you realise there are different kinds of questions. Ones where the answers are easy to find on the page are what we call **literal questions**. Others are called **inferential questions** or **evaluative questions** where you have to work out something in your head. You may need help in understanding phrases when they don't mean exactly what they say, e.g. *'He was down in the mouth.'*	Work through the section on Inferences in Chapter 5 – TRC. Explain and work through Chapter 4 – TRC to help with figurative language.
• I read OK but I am very slow. • Sometimes I am so slow I have forgotten the beginning of the sentence by the time I get to the end!	Sometimes we get too used to reading word by word because that is how we started to read. Pointing at every word might slow you down. It is probably time to move on to the next stage.	.

Cont'd

Checklist for reader to use with teacher support

Points for the reader to consider	Things to think about, things to do and targets to set for the reader	Possible Action Points for teacher and suggestions for the readers
	Phrase Reading is a good way to begin. Learning different strategies for different types of reading helps us to understand that we do not always have to read word by word. Learn how to **skim** (get your eyes working more quickly) and **scan** (find one piece of information on a page or in a book). These are the kinds of reading to use if you want to look in the paper to see when your favourite TV programme is on.	See 'Phrase Reading' in Chapter 4 of TRC See Chapter 7 of TRC 'Types of Reading' to learn how to skim and scan (find one piece of information on a page or in a book).
● I read quickly and sometimes so quickly I miss little details. Sometimes I misread important details in tests or maths problems or homework instructions.	Reading for detail is another type of reading. This is the kind of reading you need to use when every detail matters, for instance the time the plane or train takes off: **18.30** is not the same as **8.30**; **3.30 a.m.** is not the same as **3.30 p.m.** Finger pointing might suit this kind of reading. It is important to learn <u>how</u> and <u>when</u> to **read accurately**.	Chapter 7 in TRC has a section on **accurate reading**; this will help him to learn how and when to read accurately.
● I am OK if the piece of writing is short but I begin to get lost and not understand with longer pieces.	This is normal. Sometimes we move too quickly to reading that is too long or complicated. We need to learn some skills to deal with longer pieces of writing.	Chapter 5 in TRC gives you ways of helping your reader understand longer texts.

Cont'd

Checklist for reader to use with teacher support

Points for the reader to consider	Things to think about, things to do and targets to set for the reader	Possible Action Points for teacher and suggestions for the readers
● My reading seems OK when I am doing it but I don't seem to remember much by the end.	Sometimes not much sticks in our heads when we read because we do not think enough about **what** we read. Then reading is an eye exercise. Our eyes move across the page, but we have not switched on the thinking part of the brain or it switches off as we get distracted. You need ways to get your brain into a higher gear.	Chapter 8 in TRC will encourage your reader to be less passive in reading and capable of getting more out of the text. He may also need more practice with visualisation (see Chapter 9 in TRC).
● If I have a project to prepare or a lot of writing to do, I do not know where to begin.	**SQ3R** is one way of studying what you read so that you understand better **while** you read and you recall what you have read more easily **afterwards.** You might review some other targets that you have been using such as **KWL.** If you have got as far as this in this checklist you are reading at a very advanced stage. Keep up the practice. People who read become better readers! Good luck!	At this stage he is ready to use more advanced strategies that bring together a lot of the work in TRC. Use **SQ3R** in Chapter 8. Sheet 8.13 – 'Dealing with Longer Texts or Books'. Sheet 10.1, page 177 gives steps to work through, **before** you read, **while** you are reading and **after** you have finished reading.

Dealing with Longer Texts or Books

This sheet tells you what to do:

- before you read
- while you are reading
- after you have finished reading.

It is also helpful if you just want to find out more about a subject you are studying or a hobby you are interested in.

It can even be useful if you are looking for information on the Internet.

This is just a menu – pick the bits that fit with the activity you are working on at the time.

Before you read
1 Think about why you are reading and what your goal is, what kind of information you are looking for and how you are going to use it afterwards.
2 Ask yourself what you already know about this subject. This gets your brain into the right gear. Just like going somewhere – if you think about the place and remember the last time you were there, you are more likely to recognise things along the way.
3 Ask yourself what you need to find out and what you will do with the information.
• *Stages 2 and 3 are the first two stages of KWL in Chapter 8. Get your teacher to give you a target card for this if you need it.* • *It is best to make a note of these 3 questions so you do not forget them. You can keep them beside you while you are reading.*

While you read	
What do you do when you look at the text first of all?	• Practise skimming. • Look through the whole text quickly. • Notice headings, diagrams, pictures and large print. • Let your mind take in an overview of the subject. • Refer back to 'Skimming' in Chapter 7 if you need more practice in this.

Cont'd

Read it through more slowly while you think about the questions you have prepared.	• Underline or highlight key words. Some of these should jump out at you if you have prepared your brain by thinking about the subject and preparing sentences. • Use labels, Post-it®s, notes to record these key words.
Keep alert while reading, by asking questions.	• What is going on? Do I understand this? Use the traffic lights target card from Chapter 8 to make sure you stay on track while you are reading. • Make up questions as you go along. • Work with a partner and make up questions for each other. • Ask someone for help if you do get stuck.
When you finish reading	
	• Play around with the labels or Post-it®s; put them into the right order. • Take a break while your mind does some thinking. This happens even when you are not aware of it. It can happen when you are sleeping, which is why you sometimes wake up with bright ideas.
After a break,	• Turn the information into a different format. This can be any of the ways of representing information that are detailed in Chapter 7, e.g.: • mind mapping • flow diagrams • tables. Choose different formats for different kinds of information.
Look at your notes at a later date. Review how much you remember.	• Are they enough for your original purpose? • Do they give you enough information? • If they do not make complete sense go back to the original and check what is missing.

Appendix

Normal development of reading

Many think that this is the way that children develop towards fluent reading of words:

They move through phases from **logographic** to **alphabetic** to **orthographic**.

1 **Logographic** phase is the earliest stage when:
   - children guess words based on a few obvious visual features, e.g. a curvy *M* for *M*cDonalds
   - they recognise their own written names
   - letter sound links are not part of their reading knowledge
   - they cannot read new words without being told what they are.

2 **Alphabetic** phase begins to develop as:
   - children learn that letters and letter combinations are linked to sounds
   - they begin to use letter-sound links
   - they can read new words by using this code.

3 **Orthographic** phase is reached as:
   - readers become familiar with groups of letters, such as *tion* and *ology*
   - words are recognised instantly
   - letter(s)-sound combinations are used when words are unfamiliar.

These phases are not mutually exclusive. Readers may have pockets of knowledge in areas of interest or expertise. Frequently used words, absolutely regular words and rule-based words will become more quickly recognised than less frequently used and irregular words, e.g. *pneumonia, beauty, colonel,* etc.

> **Absolutely regular words** are those where there is a distinct link between letters and sounds, e.g. *stamp, act, frost.*
>
> **Rule-based words** are where a convention applies to a number of words, e.g. dropping the silent *e* before an *ing* ending, e.g. *hope + ing = hoping.*

As readers build up a 'bank' of easily recognised words they can begin to use other prompts, clues, or 'cues' in reading.

The **3-cue system** in reading, now called **Searchlights** in the National Literacy Strategy, refers to the following cues.

1. **Grapho-phonic cues** – letter/sound links: words are recognised from the letters on the page and are worked out phonically or read instantly as sight words read at sight automatically.

2. **Grammar cues** – knowledge about the structure or order of words in sentences helps readers to predict less familiar words, e.g. *The two child ... were playing with their toys.*

   A good knowledge of language and grammar will enable the early or developing reader to predict that more than one *child* will be *children* even if it is a word not read before.

3 **Meaning cues** – the early or developing reader who has a good understanding of word meanings and who has access to a good vocabulary will bring these skills to read new words, e.g. *They spent a f... on ice-cream.*

The reader with a good vocabulary may easily predict from the context that the word beginning with *f* is *fortune*; the reader who guesses *fiver* is similarly making a good guess from the overall meaning!

Good readers will access all cues as appropriate.

Reading tests

What reading tests tell you and what they don't:

There are many kinds of reading tests on the market. They include:

- single word reading
- sentence reading
- prose reading.

They test:

- accuracy
- comprehension
- speed.

Consider these points when choosing how to test and what test to use:

- Some tests require readers to read aloud. That will give an accuracy score.

- If the reader reads silently only a comprehension score can be worked out.

- If a comprehension score is based on written answers to questions, the poor writer may not do himself justice even when he has understood well.

- If comprehension questions are asked after the reader has read aloud, he may not do as well as if he read silently. For some readers reading aloud involves much more effort and creates high levels of stress.

In addition to the types of reading test described above, there are some tests which assess the ability to read **non-words**. These are designed to assess decoding of non-words which are either absolutely regular or rule based, such as **fleng**, and **boping**. These tests therefore assess decoding ability without allowing the reader to use the ability to read a word at sight. See the Helen Arkell Auditory Tests, Revised Version 2000, obtainable from the Helen Arkell Dyslexia Centre, Frensham, Farnham, Surrey, GU10 3BW Tel. no. 01252 797511.

Single word or prose reading?

Ideally use both.

Single word tests measure:

- **sight vocabulary** – those words that a reader knows automatically
- **word attack skills** – the strategies that a reader uses when he meets an unfamiliar word without any contextual clues to help him.

Single word tests therefore tap the first two searchlights in the National Literacy Strategy: phonics (sound and spelling) and **word recognition and graphic knowledge** (of letters and letter combinations).

Prose reading tests provide a measure of all four searchlights:

- grammatical knowledge
- knowledge of context
- phonics
- word recognition and graphic knowledge.

Interpreting results

Treat scores with caution!

- Results are reported as Reading Ages and sometimes as Standard Scores.

- A Standard Score can range from 85 Low Average to 115 High Average with 100 being Average.

- Results of reading tests can confuse and mislead, as reading tests do not always compare well with each other.

- Developing readers do not necessarily increase their reading ability in tandem with their chronological age. Maturity may come in fits and starts.

- Two readers can achieve identical scores but have very different reading skills and strategies. When reading prose, one reader may make many visual mistakes, omitting or substituting little words, such as *of*, *for*, *from*, etc. This may still allow him to derive meaning as he reads the longer, content words accurately. Another reader may score similarly but make mistakes with longer words which affect the amount of meaning he is able to get from the text.

- Poor readers tend to fall into one of three categories:
  - poor decoders, where comprehension might be better but can only be as good as the decoding will allow it to be
  - poor decoders and poor comprehenders
  - good decoders but poor comprehenders sometimes known as hyperlexic readers.

Some guidelines for interpreting scores

Compare single word reading with prose reading.

- If prose reading is significantly better than single word reading, consider whether the reader is over-reliant on meaning and grammar to help his reading and look at activities in *Target Reading Accuracy* to bolster his skills at word reading.

- The same is true if in a prose reading test the comprehension score exceeds the accuracy score.

- If the accuracy score is better than the comprehension score on a prose reading test, the reader needs the approach used in this book.

- Consider understanding of spoken language if reading comprehension is lower than reading accuracy. Comprehension may be poor for **spoken language**, in which case it cannot be expected in reading.

- If single word reading is significantly better than prose reading, consider whether the reader has visual tracking problems. See Chapter 5 'Visual Processing' in *Target Reading Accuracy*.

Answers

Chapter 2

Sheet 2.2, page 24

1 1 year. Reasons: teething, talking, in a buggy.
2 He did not think the smile was real. He thought she was planning something that he would not like.
3 Pushed, moved.
4 She had not had much sleep because she was disturbed by the little brother during the night.
5 He has the feeling that things are going to get worse, and has a sinking feeling inside him.
6 He does not want anyone to see him pushing the buggy because he will be embarrassed.

Sheet 2.4, pages 26–27

1 They had had their pocket money already and they would spend next week's too quickly.
2 This had happened before, probably more than once.
3 Sisters (they share a mother).
4 A brother (mother gives him pocket money also).
5 Alice should do the jobs in the living room while Mary is emptying the dishwasher and unloading the washing machine; then Alice can wash the kitchen floor while Mary is hanging out the clothes.
6 Probably Alice as she is hoovering, dusting and washing the kitchen floor.
7 She might not be sure they would complete the job or she might decide how much to give them when she saw how well the jobs were done.
8 This open-ended question can elicit a variety of responses. These answers can be challenged by asking, 'why do you think that?'. Encourage students to back up their answers.

Sheet 2.6a, page 29

1 The British become healthier during the Second World War.
2 Poor children had school meals, milk, orange juice and cod liver oil.

3 Cheese, tea and eggs.
4 1942
5 To make planes.
6 They mended them.
7 Ice cream.
8 Oranges, bananas and chocolates.
9 They got medals for collecting scrap.

Sheet 2.6b, page 30

10 a False
   b False
   c False
   d True
11 Banned.
12 Mended.
13 People ate less fat, sugar and meat.

Sheet 2.8a, page 33

1 African countries.
2 The rich countries.
3 They have to pay back the rich countries.
4 They have to borrow more money.
5 No roads, war, famine.
6 They sell goods cheaply and rich countries charge high prices for the goods they sell to the poor countries.

Sheet 2.8b, page 34

1 a False.
   b False.
   c True.
2 organisations = agencies
3 become aware = realised
4 The problem has become worse because the population has grown.
5 Bob Geldof as is mentioned in the footnote. (The question is a check on whether the reader can pick up clues from elsewhere in the text).

Sheet 2.9, page 35

people – juice – ate – small – was
scrap – from – make – nothing
stockings
playing
end
eggs

Sheet 2.10, pages 36–37

countries – back – own – borrow – worse
parts – money – wrong
agencies – government – nothing
dying – cameras – poured – late – starving
rain – food – no – changed – alive – change – buy
lowest – high – impossible
carefully – help
right – money
rich – countries – because – more – need

Chapter 4

Sheet 4.1, page 64

1 increase = make more
2 querulous = complaining
3 demotion = opposite of promotion, move to a lower rank
4 incompatible = in conflict with, incapable of both
5 morbid = unhealthy
6 penalty = punishment
7 reasonable = sensible
8 parsimonious = reluctant to spend money

Sheet 4.2, page 65

● He stayed at home.
● The glass fell on the floor.
● Take your medicine.
● The candles were still burning.
● I found the lawn mower.
● Fred broke his leg.
● Kim went out to the party.
● All my friends like new trainers.
● The band ended their tour this week.
● We will have supper.

Sheet 4.3, page 66

1 The new waitress broke the dish.
2 The Prime Minister announced lower income tax.
3 The winner of the pop contest recorded the top-selling CD.
4 A jellyfish stung the swimmer.
5 The new estate agent in town sold the house.
6 David Beckham scored the last goal.
7 The man next door looked after the garden.
8 My grandma bought my computer game.
9 Pizza House sell the best pizzas.
10 Many fans saw the film.
11 The bull chased the children.
12 The postman delivered the letter.
13 The fog slowed the lorry down.
14 Many tourists saw the city.
15 The boys in the car park washed the car.

Sheet 4.4, page 67

● The cat climbed up the tree because **the dog was chasing him.**
● Because **it had started to rain** the woman put up her umbrella.
● Because **it had been a very hot summer** there was a shortage of ice-cream.
● The pupils started to fool around because **they saw it was nearly bell time.**
● The car braked suddenly because **a child ran onto the street.**
● The footballers were furious because **they thought the referee had been unfair.**
● Because **they knew the roads would be busy** they left early for the concert.
● The computer was not working because **there was a power failure.**

Sheet 4.6, page 69

1 Lia went to the swimming pool/and after the first half hour/decided to spend most of her time/practising diving.
2 Kate's music teacher was delighted/when Kate won the top prize/in the violin section of the competition.
3 Conal wanted to act in the school play/but he knew that he had no time for rehearsals/ as his exams were starting very soon.
4 Elizabeth needed some cash/so she looked for a holiday job at Tesco/but she did not get one/as she was not old enough.
5 The AK47 gun was fired/again and again.
6 He stared/at the long line of animals/making their way/across a muddy field.
7 She wore a black cloak/and had a silver crown/on her head.
8 Everyone looked up/and saw thousands of bright stars/twinkling in the sky.
9 He waved/and a friend from school/called Dan/waved back.
10 They went on holiday/to an island/in the middle of the Pacific Ocean.

Sheet 4.7, page 70

1 All triangles have angles.   *Fact*
2 All apples are green.   *Opinion*
3 Buses are more comfortable than trains.
                                            Opinion
4 There are four seasons in the year.   *Fact*
5 Newcastle United is the best football team.
                                            Opinion
6 Planes fly in the sky   *Fact*
7 Girls are smarter than boys.   *Opinion*
8 Brazil is in South America.   *Fact*
9 Flour is an ingredient of bread.   *Fact*
10 Art is the easiest subject at school. *Opinion*

Sheet 4.8, page 71
1 Different
2 Same
3 Different
4 Same
5 Different
6 Different
7 Same
8 Different
9 Same

Sheet 4.10, page 73
The silly part of each sentence is highlighted.
- The cat went to the gate **and ate his tail**.
- The dog has four legs **and a wing on its back**.
- **A kangaroo is in a saucepan** and is playing with a baby kangaroo.
- **The coat is singing** and is hanging on the hook.
- **The egg went for a walk** after it was cooked.
- **The lorry had its supper** and then drove to London.
- The dish was white and hot **and it broke the soup**.
- The bag had a zip **with red lips**.
- The fish and chips **had a dream**.
- The boy had a red balloon **and it sang a silly song**.
- **Dry your hands with the soap** and then have your dinner.
- She stuck some stickers on her book **and then some paper clips on the roof**.

Sheet 4.12, page 76
1 Manchester United won it.
We might guess but we do not know what they won unless we have further information.
2 Trains run faster.
We do not know what they run faster than.
3 Can the taxi-driver take me there at five o'clock?
We do not know where the taxi driver will go.
4 They are arriving tonight.
We do not know who is arriving tonight.
5 Call me before my next appointment.
We do not know when the next appointment is.
6 I took his cap by mistake.
We do not know whose cap was taken.
7 Collect my jacket from one of the drycleaners in town.
We do not know which drycleaner.
8 That boy was rude to me
We do not know which boy.

Sheet 4.13, page 77
1 Will Lizzie wear her new jeans?   *Maybe*
2 Did the girls get wet?   *Yes*
3 Will Rhona have a pizza next Saturday?
Maybe
4 Will John pass his exam?   *Maybe*
5 Is Charlie's teacher pleased with him? *Maybe*
(Charlie might be wrong)

Sheet 4.14, page 78
1 Same.
2 Different.
3 Same.
4 Different.
5 Same.
6 Different.

Chapter 5

Sheet 5.1, page 88
1 This was two years before the first world war.
2 Nowadays you can go to Egypt for a holiday.
3 August is a busy month for exhibitions.
4 Mrs Smith stayed in Wales last summer.

Sheet 5.2, page 89
The first sentence is the topic sentence in paragraphs 1 and 2.

Sheet 5.3, page 90
1 C
2 D
3 A
4 B

Sheet 5.4, page 91
- Roddy found the screwdriver by the school gate.
- It was a short strong screwdriver, just the right size to fit into his pocket.
- He tried it on a hook in the cloakroom.
- It came off with no bother at all.
- Roddy smiled and put the screwdriver back into his pocket.
- Then he went on up to his classroom.
- It was late.
- He was always late.

Sheet 5.6, page 93
The King of Spain decided not to visit Holland. **While** home events may have made it difficult for him to go **at that time, it is worth noting** that he knew he would never have a better chance to go. **Secondly** the delay meant that Spain lost control of Holland. **Thirdly**, it was

very expensive to keep such a big army. **Because of this** the King of Spain decided that Holland must pay the cost. **So** Holland agreed to have a new tax. **Two years later** the new tax had not been paid.

Sheet 5.7, page 94
- Mum did not go to the shops because she was ill.
- Johnny went because his mother could not.
- He was too late for the shops because he spent too long talking to his friend.
- Mum was cross because he did not do the shopping and because he lost the money.
- She was crosser because there was no tea or biscuits for their visitors.

Sheet 5.8, page 95
Similarities: Fast food; Good value; Fill you up; Go with tomato ketchup; Easy to find.

Differences: Pizza can be vegetarian; Beefburger wheat free (without the bun); More grown-ups prefer pizza.

Sheet 5.9, page 96
1 The waiter sighed because he had wanted or expected a bigger tip.
2 The lady looked horrified because she did not like how her hair looked.
3 The fat man loosened his belt because he had eaten too much.
4 There had been a wedding.
5 They slowed down because there was an accident, road works or a break down.
6 He smiled because he had good results.

Sheet 5.10, page 97
1 Joe had been to the gym.
2 They were all going to the cinema.
3 Emily has the flu.
4 It was raining.

Sheet 5.11, page 98
Accept any appropriate diagram which contains all the key information.

Sheet 5.12, page 98

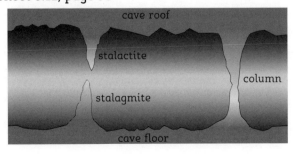

Sheet 5.13, page 99

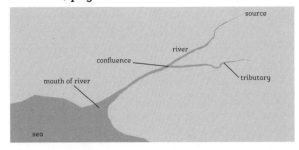

Sheet 14, page 99

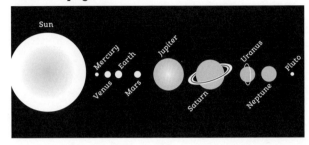

Chapter 7

Sheet 7.2, page 116
Key points:
- Levi Strauss one of largest brand name clothing companies – makes jeans / sportswear
- Levis / Dockers / Slates
- Trademark in 200 countries
- Huge staff – 1,600 in San Francisco, 30,000 world wide
- Set up by Levi Strauss, a Bavarian immigrant in 1853, died 1902
- Started with making own canvas trousers, then 20 years making work clothes
- Reinforced pockets for miners with copper rivets, patented 1873
- Business left to 4 nephews
- Levis 501, best sellers since 1890, button flies, shrink to fit, made from French blue denim
- 1936 Red tab introduced to distinguish jeans from a distance
- 108 sizes, 20 different finishes, fabrics

Sheet 7.3, page 117
1 China
2 1.5
3 120
4 16 hours

Sheet 7.5, page 119
1 Name the four largest counties in the UK.
2 List the uses of copper.
3 Translate the passage into English.
4 Name the main characters in Romeo and Juliet.

5 Imagine you are Einstein at work and write a page from his diary.
6 Describe the painting, the Mona Lisa.
7 Write down all the things that you are good at.
8 Produce a brief explanation for the beginning of the Second World War.
9 List the properties of mercury.
10 Name three types of decoration the Viking women used on clothes.

Sheet 7.7, page 121
Please note these may vary according to individual preferences; ask students to justify any variations.

1 Accurate reading.
2 Scanning/accurate reading.
3 Scanning/accurate reading.
4 Skimming/scanning.
5 Interactive reading.
6 Scanning/ accurate reading.
7 Scanning.
8 Interactive reading.
9 Scanning/accurate reading.

Chapter 8

Sheet 8.1, page 140
Highlight approximately 40 of the most important words in the following paragraph

In **many countries** the **death rate** is now **lower** than the **birth rate**. That means there are **more babies born** than **people dying**. This will make the **population rise**. In **many poor countries** it is **rising very quickly**. This will lead to **many extra people** in these countries. They will **need places to live** and **food** to eat. They need **health care** and **education**. If the population **grows too quickly** some **poor countries** will find it **difficult to cope**.

Sheet 8.2, page 141
Look at the summary and check:
a Have the main ideas been included?
b Have the readers been able to paraphrase?
c Have unnecessary details been omitted?
d Have they reduced it to the target number of words?

Suggested summary:
The Titanic made its first trip in 1912 from England to New York. The largest and most beautiful ship in the world, thought to be unsinkable, hit an iceberg on the fifth night and sank in under three hours as the sea water came in quickly.

There were lifeboats for less than half the 2,200 passengers. The crew tried to save women and children first. More than half drowned.

Poor radio contact meant only one other ship got the call for help and saved all it could find.

Sheet 8.3, page 142
Discuss with the readers why these are mistakes.

The Thomsons had just arrived at the seaside. They **opened** their sunroof in the car and left it in the car park. It was a hot and sunny day, so they put on their **gloves** and made sure they had their **umbrellas** with them. They decided to have lunch, as it was **ten o'clock** in the morning. As Mrs Thomson was a **vegetarian** they chose to go to the hamburger bar; Mr Thomson and the children ordered fish and chips and Mrs Thomson chose a **bacon butty**. The bill was for **25 pence** and Mr Thomson complained about how **expensive** eating out had become in the 21st century. They went to the beach which was lovely and **grassy**. They paddled in the water and when they discovered how **icy cold** it was they thought it would be **perfect for a swim**. They **put on all their clothes** and swam happily for the next **ten hours**. Because they were **not tired** they stopped and went home. They all agreed that they had had a **miserable** day.

Sheet 8.4a, page 143
1 a Wheat, tobacco, cotton, apples, grapes
  b Sheep and goats.
2 a Clothes like ours.
  b Black.
3 a In the country.
  b 4 or 5 rooms, flat roofs, white-washed walls, verandas with vines.

Sheet 8.4b, page 144
Three kinds
1 Percussion instruments played by *banging or striking e.g. drums*
2 Wind instruments
  a Woodwind *e.g. clarinet, flute, bassoon*
  b Brass *e.g. trumpet, trombone, horn*
  c Others *e.g. bagpipes, mouth organ*
3 Stringed instruments
  a Played with a bow *e.g. violin, cello*
  b Played by plucking *e.g. harp, guitar*

Sheet 8.5, page 145

I switched off the video and dressed for school. Tuesday is 'can't wait' day. It's straight downstairs, sneak past Mum's and Amber's **bedrooms**, and don't make a **sound** on the creaking floorboard to **wake** the dog. Pull the magazine out of the letter **box** and stuff your fingers in the letter box flap to stop it shutting with a **crash**. Then fly upstairs as fast and as quietly as you can clutching the **magazine** tight in your fist. Close your **bedroom** door without a **sound** and then breathe more easily. Open the fingers of your **hand** for your fist full of football fantasy and magic. For **Tuesday** is the day of SCORE and its free football sticker.

Sheet 8.6, page 146

- The college has formed a new orchestra and put on a concert last week.
- Dave chose to play the kettledrums.
- Kettledrums are called timpani.
- He likes to play them as they make such a loud noise.
- He does not always remember to look at the conductor.
- At the concert last week he missed a beat early in the first piece of music.
- The performance of the piece ended with a loud timpani solo.
- The composer had not written this.

Sheet 8.7, page 147

May vary, accept any response that is appropriate and supported by reasoning.

Sheet 8.8, page 148

The name '**dinosaur**' means '**terrible lizard**'. Dinosaurs were given their names because they **look** a bit **like** the lizards alive today. But dinosaurs **died out 65 million years ago**, and they were **different** from lizards and other living reptiles. They could **walk** on **straight legs** tucked under their bodies, instead of out at the side. This meant they could **walk further**, move **faster** and grow **bigger** than any other reptiles.

The best way to tell the **difference** between a reptile and an amphibian is to look at their skin. Reptiles, such as snakes and crocodiles have **dry, scaly** skin. **Amphibians** such as frogs and salamanders have **wet, smooth** skin. **Both** reptiles and amphibians have a **bony skeleton**, and their bodies are the **same temperature** as their **surroundings**. Most of them live in **warm places**.

The paragraph describes the similarities and differences between reptiles and amphibians.

Similarities: Bony skeletons; Same temperature as surroundings; Live in warm places.
Differences: Skins of reptiles dry and scaly; Skins of amphibians wet and smooth.

Sheet 8.9, page 149

Clear: Bottles and jars and their labels; Clear; Clear glass with coloured coatings.
Green: Bottles and jars and their labels; Green; Blue.
Brown: Bottles and jars and their labels; Brown.
Not allowed: Plastic or metal rings; Tops; Light bulbs; Sheet glass; Pyrex-type dishes.

Sheet 8.10b, page 151
For answer see example of mind map on Sheet 8.10c, page 152.

Chapter 9

Sheet 9.5, page 167
The correct order is:
- Megan packed her swimmers into her sports bag and set off for the outdoor pool.
- When she got there a notice on the door said 'Sorry, the heating system has failed! Half price entry today only'.
- She stood deciding for a moment or two whether she really wanted this swim.
- Well, yes, she did want a swim and it was quite a sunny day.
- Megan changed, dived in and swam half a dozen lengths.
- After a while she scrambled out of the pool shivering with cold.
- When she had dressed, she had a steaming hot cup of chocolate to drink.

Index

Acknowledgements

The publishers would like to thank the following for permission to use copyright material. Every effort has been made to trace copyright holders and to obtain their permission for the use of copyright material. The authors and publishers would welcome any information that would allow them to rectify any omissions in subsequent editions.

The Ice-cream Swipe by Elizabeth Laird (OUP, 2002), reprinted by permission of Oxford University Press; *Bob Geldof* by Charlotte Gray, used by permission of Exley Publications; *Clear and Lively Writing* by Priscilla Vail, by permission of Walker Books, USA; *Living through History: The Roman Empire* by Nigel Kelly, Rosemary Rees and Jane Shuter, reprinted by permission of Harcourt Education; *The Oxford Children's A to Z of Geography* by Dick Bateman (OUP, 2003), copyright Dick Bateman 1996; *Trees* by Linda Gamlin, by permission of Dorling Kindersley; *Life Processes and Living Things Curriculum Bank* by Frances Mackay (Scholastic 1995), copyright © Frances Mackay; *Key Stage 3 Geography Classbook* by Adam Arnell (Letts Educational 2000); *Oxford First Book of Space* by Andrew Langley (OUP, 2000), copyright © Andrew Langley 2000; *Stories for Thinking* by Robert Fisher, by permission of Nash Pollock Publishing; *Textiles Technology: the Clothing Industry* by Hazel King, reprinted by permission of Harcourt Education; pie charts, Internet hierachies, etc. *Reading for Content Book One* by Carol Einstein (Education Publishing Service); *A Visit to Greece* by Peter and Connie Roop, reprinted by permission of Harcourt Education; *Nice One Sam!* by John Goodwin (OUP, 2003), reprinted by permission of Oxford University Press; *Friday Forever* by Annie Dalton (Barrington Stoke); *First Book of Dinosaurs* by Barbara Taylor (OUP, 2001), copyright © Barbara Taylor 2001; *Societies in Change, Teacher's Resource Book* by Colin Shepherd, Chris Hinton, John Hite and Tim Lomas (John Murray 1992), reprinted by permission of HodderMurray; *Discovering Mexico* by Marion Morrison (Zoe Books).